This book was brought
to you by the

Naumes Family Foundation

Is Social Networking Beneficial to Society?

Bonnie Szumski and Jill Karson

INCONTROVERSY

ReferencePoint
Press®

San Diego, CA

For more information, contact:
ReferencePoint Press, Inc.
PO Box 27779
San Diego, CA 92198
www.ReferencePointPress.com

Picture credits:
Cover: iStockphoto.com
AP Images: 28, 59
© Sam Bloomberg-Rissman/Blend Images/Corbis: 33
© Ken Cedeno/Corbis: 12
© Akram Elsadawie/Demotix/Corbis: 38
© Monique Jacques/Corbis: 7
© Ed Kashi/Corbis: 51
© Jacqueline M. Koch/Corbis: 47
© Kari Medig/Aurora Photos/Corbis: 66
Thinkstock/iStockphoto.com: 55
Thinkstock/Photodisc: 73
© VIEW Press/Demotix/Corbis: 21

LIBRARY OF CONGRESS CATALOGING-IN-PUBLICATION DATA

Szumski, Bonnie, 1958–
    Is social networking beneficial to society? / by Bonnie Szumski and Jill Karson.
        p. cm. — (In controversy)
    Includes bibliographical references and index.
    ISBN-13: 978-1-60152-460-7 (hardback)
    ISBN-10: 1-60152-460-9 (hardback)
  1. Social networks—Juvenile literature. I. Karson, Jill. II. Title.
    HM741.S98   2013
    302.3—dc23
                                                                        2012000355

Contents

Foreword

In 2008, as the US economy and economies worldwide were falling into the worst recession since the Great Depression, most Americans had difficulty comprehending the complexity, magnitude, and scope of what was happening. As is often the case with a complex, controversial issue such as this historic global economic recession, looking at the problem as a whole can be overwhelming and often does not lead to understanding. One way to better comprehend such a large issue or event is to break it into smaller parts. The intricacies of global economic recession may be difficult to understand, but one can gain insight by instead beginning with an individual contributing factor, such as the real estate market. When examined through a narrower lens, complex issues become clearer and easier to evaluate.

This is the idea behind ReferencePoint Press's *In Controversy* series. The series examines the complex, controversial issues of the day by breaking them into smaller pieces. Rather than looking at the stem cell research debate as a whole, a title would examine an important aspect of the debate such as *Is Stem Cell Research Necessary?* or *Is Embryonic Stem Cell Research Ethical?* By studying the central issues of the debate individually, researchers gain a more solid and focused understanding of the topic as a whole.

Each book in the series provides a clear, insightful discussion of the issues, integrating facts and a variety of contrasting opinions for a solid, balanced perspective. Personal accounts and direct quotes from academic and professional experts, advocacy groups, politicians, and others enhance the narrative. Sidebars add depth to the discussion by expanding on important ideas and events. For quick reference, a list of key facts concludes every chapter. Source notes, an annotated organizations list, bibliography, and index provide student researchers with additional tools for papers and class discussion.

The *In Controversy* series also challenges students to think critically about issues, to improve their problem-solving skills, and to sharpen their ability to form educated opinions. As President Barack Obama stated in a March 2009 speech, success in the twenty-first century will not be measurable merely by students' ability to "fill in a bubble on a test but whether they possess 21st century skills like problem-solving and critical thinking and entrepreneurship and creativity." Those who possess these skills will have a strong foundation for whatever lies ahead.

No one can know for certain what sort of world awaits today's students. What we can assume, however, is that those who are inquisitive about a wide range of issues; open-minded to divergent views; aware of bias and opinion; and able to reason, reflect, and reconsider will be best prepared for the future. As the international development organization Oxfam notes, "Today's young people will grow up to be the citizens of the future: but what that future holds for them is uncertain. We can be quite confident, however, that they will be faced with decisions about a wide range of issues on which people have differing, contradictory views. If they are to develop as global citizens all young people should have the opportunity to engage with these controversial issues."

In Controversy helps today's students better prepare for tomorrow. An understanding of the complex issues that drive our world and the ability to think critically about them are essential components of contributing, competing, and succeeding in the twenty-first century.

A Communication Revolution

Social networking has transformed communication—among friends and colleagues, as well as between citizens and governments. The change has been rapid—just 15 years ago social networking was not as common or as easy as it is today. Communication analyst Clay Shirky calls this transformation "the largest increase in expressive capability in human history."[1] Shirky claims that the social networking revolution has transformed communication as much as the printing press and movable type did when it allowed more people to have access to reading material. But Shirky finds the change to be even more profound:

> "Every time a new consumer joins this media landscape a new producer joins as well, because the same equipment—phones, computers—let you consume and produce. It's as if, when you bought a book, they threw in the printing press for free; That is a huge change in the media landscape we're used to. And it's not just Internet or no Internet. We've had the Internet in its public form for almost 20 years now, and it's still changing as the media becomes more social.[2]

"*Every time a new consumer joins this media landscape a new producer joins as well, because the same equipment—phones, computers—let you consume and produce.*"[2]

— Communication analyst Clay Shirky.

Shirky's claims are not difficult to back up for anyone who has joined this media revolution. Social networking's influence ranges from the ridiculous—YouTube videos such as "Honey Badger" getting millions of hits and its tag line, "Honey Badger don't

6

care," entering teen and adult lexicon virtually within hours—to the profound—citizens in Tunisia, Iran, and Egypt using social networking to organize protests and communicate their intentions to the world.

Like all revolutions, the social networking revolution is accompanied by concerns and questions about whether the changes have wrought something better or something worse. Does the nature of friendship change, for example, when a person claims 200 people on Facebook as friends? Or does Facebook serve merely as a means to keep in touch in the same way an annual Christmas letter might be sent to both friends and acquaintances to let them know they are in one's thoughts. Are the so-called Twitter Revolutions in the Middle East (so-called because the use of the popular networking tool seems a significant way to update events in real time) really any different from revolutions in the past? After all, the same discontent fuels the new revolutions as it did the old—just a different media form is being used.

Egyptian protesters, singing in Cairo's Tahrir Square in 2011, use cell phones to capture the momentous events taking place in their country. Pictures and video taken by ordinary people and posted on social networking sites allowed the world a close-up view of revolutions throughout the Middle East.

What seems clearly different is that the audience is larger than ever before, and the message—personal, political, international—is heard around the world even faster. And, as Shirky and others believe, we are all producing the message, all the time. Any individual can now publish a song, a book, make a comment, and participate in an ongoing dialogue with the world. The power once held by publishers and creators of media has been diminished. The impact of this will clearly be left to future generations.

What Are the Origins of the Social Networking Debate?

While driving off-road motorcycles in a remote location in Baja, California, Tom's motorcycle stopped. His friends grouped around him to try to figure out what had made the motorcycle quit working, but to no avail. The group had no choice but to abandon the motorcycle and head on to their hotel for the night, 100 miles away. While at the hotel, Tom got on a popular off-road motorcycle site, AVRider.com, to query other riders about what could have happened to his motorcycle. Within the hour, several people with the identical motorcycle posted solutions, and several riders in Baja offered tows, places to stay, and tools to help fix it. Calling upon one of these fellow riders, Tom got a ride back to the site of his motorcycle, went to the home of his newfound friend, and repaired his motorcycle. The group was up and riding to their next destination by the following day.

Zeke had never made sushi and was unsure of how to make sticky rice. He found a YouTube video on the Internet with someone showing the steps from beginning to end. The video also demonstrated how to roll sushi rolls and make other items.

Gail was living in a small, rural town when her husband was diagnosed with Parkinson's disease. With her husband sullen, uncommunicative, and in denial over his symptoms and the severity of the disease, Gail found few people, other than her husband's physician, who could communicate with her about her worries. She found a Parkinson's support group on the web, which helped her to find women going through similar battles, and, to her surprise, with similar issues regarding their husbands' reactions to the disease. Gail found the site a helpful outlet when she needed information and encouragement.

John, 17, regularly plays a popular online video game. He connects with dozens of other users via a live chat program in which many other teen players communicate on strategies as well as compete with one another in real time.

Changed Lives

These are just a few examples of social networking and how it has changed people's lives. It has become a way of communicating and solving problems both large and small—in so many ways that it would be impossible to name them all. But one thing is certain; such communication was not possible even 15 years ago.

Social networking sites are virtual places on the Internet where people of usually like-minded interests log on to chat, play a game, or gather information. Most, such as MySpace, Facebook, and Bebo, allow users to create a profile and to gather other users to make a list of contacts that they can share information with on the site. Within this network of chosen individuals, the group can maintain and share content.

Since their introduction in the mid-1990s, millions of people have joined social networking sites worldwide. Three of the world's most well-known brands are Facebook, YouTube, and Wikipedia. In 2010 users around the world spent over 110 billion minutes on social network and blog sites. However, social networking had to overcome a number of hurdles,

"It seemed a lot easier to speak on the computer, even though I couldn't type very well. I remember having three or four conversations going at once with different friends."[4]

— Dan Conger, an early user of instant messaging.

both technological and cultural, before it would become a dominant part of the social landscape.

Computerized Bulletin Boards

In the early 1980s, the concept of social networking began with the idea of a bulletin board. As former IBM employee Ward Christensen explains, "At our club meetings, we had a cork board and push-pin bulletin board, with 3x5 cards with things like Need ride to next meeting . . . etc., So I came up with the idea of computerizing that."[3] This concept, called CBBS (Computerized Bulletin Board System), is a virtual area where users post public messages. Although limited in use and scope, the concept began to broaden to other groups who wanted to post messages to other members. The idea expanded to include the ability to converse with one another, replying and responding to each other's posts. The concept took off once large Internet service providers (ISPs) such as Compuserve, AOL, Prodigy, Earthlink, and others began to expand the bulletin board concept to more users.

One of the earliest of these virtual bulletin boards was BHI (Beverly Hills Internet), started in 1995. A user on BHI could choose one of several areas (called neighborhoods) and post with like users. The concept grew quickly, and the site garnered thousands of users. The name changed to GeoCities, and in 1997 had a population of more than a million members. As the sites grew, they encountered problems with memory and equipment. In fact, early social networking was hindered by limitations with hardware, including the capacity of servers and the need for constant maintenance.

> "I remember people competing to see how many 'friends' they could accumulate [gather] and how quickly, and tracking how many 'friends' they shared in common with other 'friends.'"[5]
>
> — Olivia Ma, former Harvard student.

But technology was constantly evolving and improving the usability and reliability of social networking sites. Another successful outgrowth of GeoCities was Classmates.com, founded in 1995. The site was founded on the idea that people would want to find and message their former classmates. Tens of millions of users signed up for the site, but again, technological issues arose.

Fakesters

Hand in hand with the increasing contact between individuals on the Internet went fears of what that contact, especially for minors, could mean. While adults seemed to be somewhat immune to "fakesters," people posting false identities on the Internet, impressionable young people seeking connections online could hook up with adults posing as children. As early as 1993, a case emerged that highlighted the darker side of social networking. A 10-year-old boy, George Burdynski, was reported missing in Brentwood, Maryland. His disappearance was linked to two men who were luring boys online to meet and force them to pose for pornographic photos. They posted such photos on a private bulletin board service to distribute pornography and hook up with boys for sex. Burdynski was never found, but the event showcased how vulnerable children were on the Internet, and how predators now seemed to have an entirely different, and more secretive, way to commit

Instant messaging, which allows real-time chats online, was introduced in the late 1990s. It became popular as a means of communication in the workplace (pictured) and at one point even surpassed e-mail as a means of communicating with coworkers and clients.

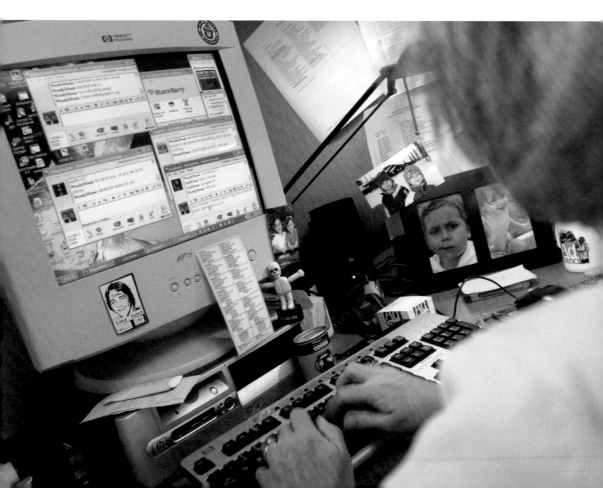

crimes. As new technologies developed, adapting their use to protect children continued to be an area of concern.

Instant Messaging and Further Refinements

The next development on the social networking horizon, called instant messaging, was released in 1997 by AOL. The initial release was limited to people who knew each other's e-mail addresses and who also subscribed to AOL. Instant messaging allowed for someone online to be pinged by another AOL user online for a real-time chat. Early instant messaging was somewhat cumbersome, as the lag time between messages was affected by the speed of the Internet connection. Still, people caught on to and enjoyed this type of conversation more than the telephone. Dan Conger, one early adopter, remembers, "It seemed a lot easier to speak on the computer, even though I couldn't type very well. I remember having three or four conversations going at once with different friends."[4]

Using a combination of technologies and attempting to learn from the failures of other sites, SixDegrees.com took social networking further in 1997. The site acted more like the social networking sites of today. It allowed users to set up an account and create a profile with likes and dislikes. Although the site was popular, it was plagued by an inability to make a profit. ISPs like AOL could charge people for access to the Internet, but early social networking sites had a hard time getting people to pay for use. Such sites had to rely on advertisers. Though common today, advertisers were not quite comfortable with the new Internet model and were reluctant to spend money on such sites that offered only a slim chance that users would purchase their products. With the advertising model still in its infancy, and hardware still very expensive, new social networking sites had a difficult time paying for hardware, bandwidth, and site managers. Many sites cut back on costs by using volunteers to manage equipment problems.

Building on the same concept as SixDegrees—making and being able to communicate with a circle of friends—Friendster was launched in 2003. Friendster attracted 3 million registered users within six months. Unfortunately, the site's numbers dragged down its efficiency, and the site's servers were overwhelmed and

A New Sense of Community

In the book *More than MySpace: Teens, Librarians, and Social Networking*, Robyn M. Lupa introduces the concept that, instead of creating disconnection among its users, social networking is actually creating more community. She argues that people's need to belong is most often satisfied by family, school, work, places to worship, and clubs and civic organizations. But social networking is allowing even more connection, albeit digitally. Lupa quotes technology writer Trent Batson as arguing:

> The social Web is an outward sign of an inner human social reality and drive. And it works well, surprisingly well. Good social sites can serve to remind you of friends you knew long ago or colleagues you've lost touch with. They support a new, or very old, human conversation, so we know what those in our "small town on the Web" are doing, how to get a hold of them from anywhere in the world, and remind you of their title or of their own group of colleagues—as part of a *conversation* instead of a Web search.

Quoted in Robyn M. Lupa, ed., *More than MySpace: Teens, Librarians, and Social Networking*. Santa Barbara, CA: ABC Clio, 2009.

plagued with shutdowns and slow load-ups.

Although beset by myriad problems, all of these early sites proved that people would not only accept the concept of communicating digitally but actually grow to prefer it over meeting personally and/or talking on the telephone. The idea of communicating by posting to a large group of friends, rather than communicating with each one individually, appealed to both young and older people. Social networking was accepted early by many people, but hardware issues kept it from being universally adopted. By 2005, with the necessary technology in place to support the platforms, social networking sites would achieve blockbuster status with the launch of MySpace and Facebook.

MySpace and Facebook

When MySpace came on the scene in 2003, Friendster was reporting a membership of about 27 million users. While Friendster allowed people to display personal data and upload photographs, MySpace allowed users to customize pages. Millions of teens and young adults quit Friendster and flocked to MySpace. By 2006 MySpace membership was growing by about 250,000 members a day. The site became critically important to teens as a social hangout, much like congregating at a shopping mall or in a park had been in the past. The difference, clearly, was the fact that many of these contacts were people the teens barely knew. The new social contacts were redefining the way teens, at first, and ultimately everyone, would choose to interact with one another. The tremendous success and growth of MySpace, however, was nothing compared with that of another site that began in 2004—Facebook.

In 2003 Mark Zuckerberg was a student at Harvard University when he got the idea to launch Facebook. Familiar with other sites at the time, Zuckerberg wanted to take the popular address book provided to all students at Harvard and make it digital so that students could post information about and contact each other. Harvard did not like Zuckerberg's idea about using Harvard's address book online and quickly shut it down.

Undaunted, Zuckerberg came up with the idea of The Facebook and launched it on his own website in February 2004. Again, it was just for college students and initially gained membership simply by word of mouth. The site had 1,500 users in just one day. The site continued to gain in popularity, gaining 4,000 members in two weeks. Former Harvard student Olivia Ma, recalls, "I remember people competing to see how many 'friends' they could accumulate [gather] and how quickly, and tracking how many 'friends' they shared in common with other 'friends.'"[5]

Since these humble beginnings, Facebook has climbed in popularity in the United States and in many other parts of the world. Early on, Zuckerberg expanded the user base to include teenagers and adults, and the site has become a phenomenon. The verb "to Facebook" is now common lexicon among Americans. The site's easy-to-use format, as well as the ability to maintain and find new "friends" continuously and keep up with them in the virtual world, has made it the most popular site of its kind. Facebook membership continues to grow. In 2005 the site had 1 million members. In 2011 that number had increased to 750 million. The average user contributes 90 pieces of content to the site each month. And Facebook is not just a US phenomenon, 70 percent of its users are outside the United States.

Vulnerable Youth

With social networking accelerating so rapidly in 2005 and 2006, worries over privacy and the vulnerability of young users began to grow as well. The media reported acts of cybercrime, including bullying, slander, and loss of privacy. Especially worrisome was the fact that teenagers did not seem to understand that information sent on the Internet remained public for a long time. Items posted on Facebook pages could be viewed by parents, teachers, and other individuals, becoming a permanent part of a young person's history.

The 2006 case of Megan Meier highlighted a type of crime that would have been unthinkable before the days of online social networking. Megan was a 13-year-old who was taunted and harassed online by a friend's mother, Lori Drew, who wanted to find out if Megan had been spreading rumors about her daughter. Drew, who created a fake profile on MySpace as a boy named Josh, initially befriended and later romanced Megan, then taunted her with nasty online messages. These messages included such cruel thoughts as "the world would be a better place without you."[6] Crushed and vulnerable, Megan ultimately committed suicide by hanging herself shortly before her fourteenth birthday.

The media seized on the case because it seemed to illustrate many problems on the Internet, including the vulnerability of teenagers to online taunts. A whole new venue had opened up to bullies—and it could be done in secret, virtually anonymously, allowing for a teen's online "friends" to join in the attack. In addition, the mother's ability to create a completely false profile and impersonate someone else again focused public attention on the safety of giving out information on the Internet.

Changing Relationships

As people move away from live-person contact and connect more via the Internet, how this new contact defines friendship is under study. Many feel that this changing social landscape will have a profound impact on society. As early as 2002 the *Journal of Social Issues* reported that social networking sites appeared to reduce loneliness and improve well-being, especially for people who may have difficulty communicating in traditional settings, such as individuals with Asperger's syndrome. A 2006 survey reported that Facebook users mostly use the site to stay in touch with people they meet in the real world. One 2007 study by researchers at Michigan State University found that members primarily use the site to connect with people they already know and see on a regular basis as opposed to finding new people to meet. Although these relationships were not always deep and meaningful friendships, they were often ways to stay in contact with friends that had been made through school or a hobby. A 2010 study at the University of Virginia found a similar result among teens. According to psychologist Amori Yee Mikami, who authored the study, adolescents primarily use social networking sites to maintain established friendships and not to converse with strangers. Mikami also found that participants who were better adjusted in their teens were more likely to continue their use of social media as they grew older. Other research is not as reassuring. A 2010 study by the Mental Health Foundation found that 53 percent of 18- to 34-year-olds felt depressed or lonely because they spent too much time communicating online and not enough in person.

Just the fact that social networking sites are so universally

"OWS [Occupy Wall Street] might be the perfect example of how social media can start a revolution."[7]

— Kimling Lam, former television reporter and employee of Meltwater, a media monitoring service.

used has allowed researchers to mine their data to study the public's habits, from their online purchasing habits to something as personal as how and why they choose a mate. Studying people's personal habits is becoming easier, and is allowing marketers and other savvy entrepreneurs new ways to sell products and services tailored to these habits. One example is that coupon manufacturers use online shopping habits and online profiles, such as those posted on LinkedIn and Facebook, to send coupons directly to consumers. Such coupons might include users' hobbies and where they eat dinner with friends. These social networking trends, however, seem small compared to the way they have influenced the political arena—especially with the explosive growth of texting.

From Blog to Fame

The American sitcom called *$#*! My Dad Says* aired in the 2010–2011 television season. It was based on a popular Twitter feed started by 28-year-old Justin Halpern. Halpern blogged about the eccentric and oftentimes inexplicable and offensive things that his 73-year-old father would say. His blog quickly gained over 1 million followers who enjoyed father Sam Halpern's sarcastic quotes. One example, "Son, no one gives a sh*t about all the things your cell phone does. You didn't invent it, you just bought it. Anybody can do that." The feed took on a life of its own, and Halpern was offered a book deal and the television show, which starred William Shatner as Halpern's father. Halpern's story proved that traditional publishing and media outlets, in need of refreshing and new inspiration for their lineups, were looking toward social networking sites to provide it. Halpern's story has since led to other projects for other bloggers.

Quoted in Patrick Phillips, "Justin Halpern: 'Sh*t My Dad Says' Guy Worries About Media," *I Want Media*, June 29, 2010.

Impact on Politics

Texting was a little-known application when it was introduced in Nokia's first mobile phones in 1993. Usage boomed as people discovered the ease and relative lack of personal commitment sending text messages allowed. Texting's private impact, however, would soon pale against the ways it could be used to spread geopolitical events with lightning speed. In 2001 a texting revolution in the Philippines contributed to the ouster of leader Joseph Estrada. After Philippine congressional loyalists voted to set aside key evidence that proved Estrada should be impeached, angry Philippine citizens began a protest at a major public crossroads in Manila. Many of the protesters learned of the event through text messages that read "Go 2 EDS. Wear blk." Over a million people arrived at the protest, effectively stopping all traffic from getting in and out of downtown Manila. Almost 7 million text messages were sent before the protest, and they sealed Estrada's fate. Estrada blamed the texting generation for his ouster. The event marked the first time social media played a pivotal role in world events. It would by no means be the last.

The 2008 US presidential campaign proved fertile ground to illustrate the role social networking could play in domestic politics. Barack Obama and other political candidates used Facebook, MySpace, Twitter, YouTube, and other forms of social media as a means of communicating with young voters, who had always been the ones to quickly adapt to new technologies. More than a quarter of voters under the age of 30 reported that they followed the election via social networking sites. Obama's early adoption of the new social networking opportunities was largely credited with his ability to garner roughly two-thirds of the younger vote. Obama continues to use the sites as a way to communicate directly with the public. During the US debt crisis, Obama asked the public to send Twitter messages to members of Congress urging a balanced approach to ending the crisis. Recent world events in the Middle East, including a revolution in Egypt, prove that social networking will be used in new ways to allow ordinary citizens to make meaningful and significant changes in the world.

Just as social networking seems to have transformed traditional politics, it also appears to be gaining in popularity as a means for the average citizen to gain political prominence. The Tea Party movement, for example, began as a blog in 2003 and is now a significant conservative political force. The group was largely ignored by the mainstream media outlets even as it gained momentum in the social networking arena. In 2008, when housewife Stacy Mott, a new mother, began her blog "Smart Girl Politics," protesting government bailouts of banks, she single-handedly started a campaign that would go national and ring true for many Americans. Mott's blog became a place for like-minded individuals to meet and plan political rallies.

Hundreds of similar blogs were started in support of the new movement, which came to be known as the Tea Party. With no budget for traditional direct mail campaigns or pamphleteering, Facebook became a central gathering spot to organize and announce activities. By 2009, after only a single year, 2,000 Tea Party–related Facebook pages could be found on the Internet. One member consolidated these disparate pages, and the group began calling itself Tea Party Patriots. The party quickly moved to Twitter, where members could call town hall meetings and rallies. The movement was truly grassroots—no single unifying entity led the party—and it remained the voice of thousands of Americans who had used social networking to gain a political presence.

Yet while the Tea Party largely formed on the Internet, traditional media outlets did, in fact, spread the word and give it the prominence it has now achieved. Once newspapers such as the *New York Times* and the *Wall Street Journal* began to write about the movement's activities, its actions and rallies were fully covered, and the movement's foibles, such as racist computer-altered images of President Barack Obama, went national. The exposure both galvanized the hard-core conservative members while alienating people who were more middle-of-the-road.

Occupy Wall Street

Yet another movement tested the ability of social networking to enter into the national political scene. In 2011 the Occupy Wall

Street movement gained momentum, again beginning with a social networking tool. This one is called a hashtag—a tag embedded in a message posted on Twitter, consisting of a word within the message prefixed with a hash sign (#). The hashtag was posted on Twitter by an activist group called AdBusters on July 13, 2011. It called for protesters to occupy Wall Street on September 17. One day after September 17, tweets about the movement increased 850 percent in 24 hours. Protesters flooded Facebook, Twitter, and YouTube to share photos, video, and to express their thoughts. Again, mainstream media largely ignored the burgeoning movement, mostly because it seemed to lack an organized cause.

As with the Tea Party, media attention grew with the group's increasingly visible presence on social media sites. Starting on Wall Street in New York City, "Occupy" movements expanded across the country in many large cities, all fueled by social networking sites. Cities that tried to extract the protesters by force were con-

Demonstrators take part in an Occupy Wall Street march in New York in 2011. The movement built momentum nationwide largely through exposure on various social networking sites.

demned on social networking sites. The day-to-day activities of the protesters, and the police and National Guard attempts to extract them, began to appear in national newspapers with regularity. National figures such as President Obama and former House Speaker Newt Gingrich commented on the movement's goals, saying that it clearly was expressing the frustration felt by thousands of out-of-work and disgruntled Americans.

Added Momentum for Social Movements

While these grassroots movements have always been a part of American politics, the swiftness by which they have gained momentum seems unarguably due to readily available social networking sites to spread the message. As Kimling Lam of the media monitoring service Meltwater remarks: "The evolution from a blog with a Twitter hashtag to in-person events all over the globe with mainstream media coverage in fewer than four months exemplifies the power of social media. OWS [Occupy Wall Street] might be the perfect example of how social media can start a revolution."[7]

Clearly, social networking is firmly entrenched in modern culture. Its use is outpacing not only the ability of social scientists to assess its effects but also the development of rules and laws to govern its use. In the years ahead, lawmakers, scholars, and many other observers will weigh in about whether social networking improves the quality of people's lives and how to manage the wide accessibility of so much personal information.

Facts

- **About 70 percent of Facebook users are outside the United States.**

- **The world now spends over 110 billion minutes a year on social networking and blog sites.**

- **Former Massachusetts Republican governor Mitt Romney announced his presidential bid on April 11, 2011, in an online video.**

CHAPTER TWO

Is Social Networking Changing the Nature of Relationships?

Evolutionary biologists, psychologists, and others have long noted that humans are inherently social beings. John Cacioppo is a University of Chicago research psychologist who has spent 30 years researching the power of social connection—and the severe emotional and even physical problems associated with loneliness and social isolation. In his book *Loneliness: Human Nature and the Need for Social Connection* Cacioppo writes that the notion that humans are wired to be social is no longer contestable and that "when people are asked what pleasures contribute most to happiness, the overwhelming majority rate love, intimacy, and social affiliation above wealth or fame, even above physical health."[8] Cacioppo goes on to say that being socially isolated is associated with high levels of stress and anxiety and carries a health impact comparable to smoking, obesity, or even high blood pressure.

The psychologist John Bowlby, known for his pioneering work in child development, believes that these health effects and other negative sensations associated with loneliness evolved to protect the individual from the dangers of remaining alone. As Bowlby writes, "To be isolated from your band and, especially when young, to be isolated from your particular caretaker is fraught with the greatest danger. Can we wonder then that each animal is equipped with an instinctive disposition to avoid isolation and to maintain proximity?"[9] Many experts believe that social networking technology—like virtually all communications technology—fulfills these deep human impulses to be connected with others.

June Cohen, director of media at the TED Conference, contends that today's social networking, by allowing people to stay connected to their community near and far, mimics the intensely social tribal societies from which humans evolved:

> As soon as [communications] technology became available to us, we began instinctively re-creating the kinds of content and communities we evolved to crave. Our ancestors lived in small tribes, keeping their friends close and their children closer. They quickly shared information that could have life-or-death consequences. They gathered round the fire for rituals and storytelling that bonded them as a tribe. And watch us now. The first thing most of us do with a new communications technology is to gather our tribe around us—e-mailing photos to our parents, friending our kids on Facebook.[10]

Today, social networking tools greatly facilitate people's ability to communicate with a wide array of friends, family members, and acquaintances. With so many people meeting and conversing online, however, some observers worry that social networking technology may be supplanting face-to-face interaction and otherwise changing the way people forge and maintain relationships. Others laud the social connectivity that social networking fosters and believe that the psychological benefits conferred outweigh any potential drawbacks.

Endless Connections

Twitter, Facebook, and other social networking tools enable users today to overcome real-life boundaries, such as time or space, and

"Honest Signals"

According to Will Reader at Sheffield Hallam University in the United Kingdom, real friendships will always be forged through real-world meetings, which help build the skills that are crucial to fostering authentic, meaningful relationships. According to Reader, personal interaction is necessary to discern what he calls "honest signals," such as facial expressions, physical gestures, or body posture, for example. Reader explains that online communication removes these valuable social cues that are necessary to determine whether a person is a true friend. As Reader states: "It's very easy to be deceptive on the internet." It may also contribute to antisocial behavior such as cyberbullying. While bullying was common before the advent of social networking, Facebook, MySpace, and other social media appear to have amplified the problem by making it easier for a bully to harass or threaten another person via the computer screen—which is virtually bereft of Reader's so-called "honest signals."

Quoted in James Randerson, "Social Networking Sites Don't Deepen Friendships," *Guardian*, September 10, 2007. www.guardian.co.uk.

maintain connections to a virtually unlimited number of people regardless of their physical location. Consequently, today's social networking tools enable individuals to connect with many more people than in real life.

According to a body of research, however, there appears to be a limit to the number of people with whom a single individual can maintain a stable, meaningful relationship. In the early 1990s, a British anthropologist named Robin Dunbar studied human group behavior at the Evolutionary Psychology and Behavioural Ecology Research Group at Liverpool University. Dunbar found that the average human being has a friendship circle of approximately 150 individuals and a more intimate clique of 12 people.

Dunbar's number of 150 has been used to study social networking communities and assess how online socializing affects real-life relationships. Much of the research has confirmed that even though the number of friends people have on social networking sites can be massive, the number of close friends is about the same as in the real world. Researcher Will Reader of Sheffield Hallam University in the United Kingdom reports that while some people have hundreds or even thousands of friends on Facebook or other social networking sites, people typically have, on average, five close friends. These and other findings suggest that the majority of Facebook "friends" can be classified as "weak ties." To some observers, the preponderance of weak ties suggests that social networking sites foster mostly shallow, impersonal relationships. As *New York Times* executive editor Bill Keller puts it: "For some people, Facebook creates a kind of friendship that is more superficial than the kind that grows out of hours spent together in one another's company. . . . It also makes it possible to feel like you have a meaningful social life when, in reality, you are missing something."[11]

On the other hand, proponents of social networking contend that these so-called weak ties are extremely valuable resources because they enable individuals to connect with a wide array of strangers with whom they can share information, ideas, and personal experiences. In this way, weak ties greatly expand a person's ability to solve problems by increasing the diversity of opinion available. Morten Hansen, a professor of management at the University of California at Berkeley, argues that weak ties are more important than strong ties and actually represent the real value of social networking. As he writes in his book *Collaboration*:

> Weak ties can prove much more helpful in networking, because they form bridges to worlds we do not walk within. Strong ties, on the other hand, tend to be worlds we al-

"We're not replacing everyday personal social networks with everyday online social networks. That's not the way it works. We're not substituting online for offline. We're augmenting."[18]

— Keith Hampton, assistant professor of communications at the University of Pennsylvania in Philadelphia.

ready know; a good friend often knows many of the same people and things we know. They are not the best when it comes to searching for new jobs, ideas, experts, and knowledge. Weak ties are also good because they take less time. It's less time consuming to talk to someone once a month (weak tie) than twice a week (strong tie). People can keep up quite a few weak ties without them being a burden.[12]

Shared Interests and Ideas

Whether they are weak or strong ties, the reasons that individuals cultivate these online connections are endless. Sites such as MySpace or Facebook, for example, allow users to create message boards, or groups of people with similar interests, such as taste in music, an interest in football, or political views, for example. Some use social networking tools to form support groups to communicate with others who are dealing with issues, such as physical ailments, similar to their own. Tamaryn Stevens, who was diagnosed with kidney disease when she was 10, uses Livewire, a social networking site that was created for young people with serious illnesses. As Stevens relates: "It's hugely beneficial. Especially the days you feel [down] in real social situations like school and things like that. You go home and you go into *Livewire* and there're people to talk to and it makes your day that much better."[13]

WebTribes, an online network of support websites, similarly provides access to a range of communities for patients dealing with anxiety, obsessive compulsive disorder, depression, and other psychological disorders. As one user reports: "I never thought there could be anyone out there who felt like I did until I found DepressionTribe. I know this site has helped me, and many others in this world, to find peace, support, and common ground with one another."[14] By giving these individuals access to a supportive community, sites like Livewire and WebTribes may be creating a sense of unity and improving the quality of life for many.

"On social networking sites such as Facebook, we think we will be presenting ourselves, but our profile ends up as somebody else—often the fantasy of who we want to be."[23]

— Sherry Turkle, MIT professor and author of *Alone Together: Why We Expect More from Technology and Less from Each Other.*

Social networking also aids people with conditions that may prevent or impede socialization in real life. For example, communication via an electronic screen may make it easier for shy people to open up and express themselves. As one observer notes, "No one stutters or stammers on Twitter."[15] For people with physical disabilities, social networking may foster free self-expression and the ability to mingle with many people, something that might be difficult in the offline world. According to Guy Lecky-Thompson, the author of several books on computers and technology issues, "Online communication can help those with dysfunctional syndromes achieve a level of social interaction previously difficult or impossible. For some people, interaction with crowds is made easier if they do not actually feel the physical immersion. Such sites also provide those isolated by disability or environment with a rich and fulfilling social life."[16]

Members of Parents and Friends of Lesbians and Gays, also known as P-FLAG, march in a gay pride parade in St. Louis, Missouri. Social networking sites have helped gay teens and their families connect with like-minded people who can offer support and acceptance.

A Sense of Belonging

For people who do not have mainstream interests or lifestyles, the anonymity of social networking may offer additional benefits. Gay teens, for example, may experience harassment or discrimination at school or in their local community: According to Parents and Friends of Lesbians and Gays (P-FLAG), an overwhelming majority of gay youth report that they are frequently subjected to homophobic remarks from other students. Connecting with other gay teens via social networking sites can reinforce a message of acceptance and offer these individuals the opportunity to express themselves freely with perhaps a much wider variety of like-minded people than would ordinarily be encountered in real life.

That social networking facilitates communication between like-minded individuals and fosters feelings of belonging is incontrovertible. At the same time, parents and other observers have noted that social networks can also forge dubious relationships that may not have developed face to face—and which may allow troubling behavior to go unchecked. For example, young women struggling with anorexia or bulimia can easily hook into a burgeoning online subculture of individuals who not only suffer from the disease but also encourage others to stay ill. These networks, which are easily accessed by young girls, may feature photos of emaciated models as "thinspiration" and offer tips to suppress hunger or hide evidence of their disease from caregivers. Other extreme examples include domestic hate groups that recruit online or the global jihadist movement that brings like-minded individuals together in cyberspace and encourages terrorist activity through online tutorials on building bombs or firing surface-to-air-missiles, for example.

Effect on Real-Life Encounters

Another potentially negative aspect of social networking relates to the inordinate amount of time that many individuals spend online. Today, Americans report spending approximately 25 percent of their time on social networking sites, and some studies put this figure much higher. Some experts worry that this growing tendency to spend so much time in the cyber-world impedes real-life relationships, although to date, much of the research has reached contradictory conclusions.

In one survey of 2,000 college undergraduates, one in seven students reported that social networking sites increased their feelings of isolation and loneliness, despite an expanded circle of casual social connections online. As psychiatrist Amir Afkhami at George Washington University comments, "Individuals recede to this virtual world of having these kinds of virtual friendships and connections. But they don't receive the same sort of supportive en-

Narcissism

Jean Twenge, a professor of psychology at San Diego State University and author of the book *The Narcissism Epidemic*, has conducted extensive research on the culture of narcissism. Twenge reviewed college student responses to the Narcissistic Personality Inventory, a test that measures narcissistic traits such as lack of empathy for others, over a 25-year period, finding that levels of narcissism have never been higher. Many observers contend that MySpace, Facebook, and other social networking technologies are responsible for the rising rates of narcissism and attention-getting behaviors. As Scott Caplan, associate professor of communications at the University of Delaware, puts it: "Facebook 'friends' should really be called 'fans.' What I put up there [on Facebook] is narcissistic stuff for my fans, like saying that I had box seats for a Phillies game. This is a narcissistic enterprise . . . [and] it may be becoming more important to impress people with the minute details of your life" than to engage in real communication.

Quoted in Marcia Clemmitt, "Social Networking," *CQ Researcher*, September 17, 2010, www .cqpress.com.

vironment that you do when you have a real connection to a real living, breathing individual."[17] Another study, by social psychologist Robert Kraut at Carnegie Mellon University in Pittsburgh, similarly found that individuals who relied on online social media to communicate with others increased their depression and feelings of isolation.

At the same time, a body of research suggests that most people use online tools to communicate with someone they already know, which actually reduces depression. As Keith Hampton, an assistant professor of communication at the University of Pennsylvania in Philadelphia, explains, "We're not replacing everyday personal social networks with everyday online social networks. That's not the way it works. We're not substituting online for offline. We're augmenting."[18]

Other research appears to support this view. A 2010 Pew Internet study found that most people still prefer face-to-face encounters as opposed to online exchanges. Another study that appeared in 2010 in the journal *American Behavioral Scientist* found that heavy Internet users had the most friends. As Barry Wellman, who cowrote the study, says, "The more people are online, the more they are relating to everyone else. . . . The mythology we have is that people used to spend whole days hanging around community—like the bar at Cheers. They didn't. They stayed home. If we switch from television to social networking sites, it's a switch toward sociability—not away from it."[19]

By these measures, online social networking is just an extension of real-world social interaction, which remains as popular as ever. At the same time, many critics charge that the constancy of online connection degrades the face-to-face encounters that are so important to maintaining stable relationships.

Constant Distraction

Today, young people between the ages of 11 and 14 spend on average 73 minutes a day texting. Older users, too, appear to be spending a massive amount of time texting and, in general, using other social networking tools in a way that detracts from how they communicate in the real world: Many teenagers are so preoccupied with texting or updating their status that they fail to engage in real-world conversation, even as they sit next to one another at sporting events or the school cafeteria, for example. It is also not uncommon for parents and children to text during family meals or other events, and many children and teenagers have complained that it is difficult to get the attention of multitasking parents. Hannah, a high school junior, describes how her mother's texting habits impede normal conversation when her mother comes to pick her up from school or dance class: "The car will start; she'll be driving still looking down, looking at her messages, but still no hello."[20]

In addition, the new wave of social networking focuses on being fast. Exchanges, therefore, are often short and superficial, with thoughts distilled down to the most rudimentary nouns and verbs. Twitter, for example, is actually based on the idea that fewer words are better; this hugely popular microblogging service allows its users to send and read only short posts of 140 characters. Some experts worry that this characteristic of Twitter and other social media may be degrading young peoples' ability to understand emotional nuances and express themselves in meaningful ways. Sherry Turkle, a professor and psychologist at MIT, is among those who believe that this fundamental change in the way people communicate is harming interpersonal skills and self-introspection:

> Today's adolescents have no less need than those of previous generations to learn empathic skills, to think about their values and identity, and to manage and express their feelings. They need time to discover themselves and to think. . . . The text driven world of rapid response does not make self-reflection impossible but does little to cultivate it. When interchanges are reformatted for the small screen and reduced to the emotional shorthand of emoticons, there are necessary simplifications."[21]

Others feel that such concerns are exaggerated and that texting and other forms of electronic communication are a fast and convenient way for individuals to stay connected. Danah Boyd is a research professor in media, culture, and communication at

New York University who examines the dynamics of social networks in society. According to Boyd, rapid online communication—albeit shallow at times—serves a social purpose by fulfilling a teenager's inherent need to know what's going on. As Boyd writes: "Teen conversations may appear completely irrational, or pointless at best. 'Yo, wazzup?' 'Not much, how you?' may not seem like much to an outsider, but this is a form of social grooming. It's a way of checking in, confirming friendships, and negotiating social waters."[22]

Creating an Online Identity

No matter how an individual chooses to interact with others in the cyber-world, he or she must create an online identity, and indeed, social networking sites offer new possibilities for experimenting with personal identity. On Facebook, for example, users can create any profile they want—writing, editing, deleting, and rewriting their personal narratives. Many users have admitted to

A student doing homework in the library takes a break to text a friend. Texting and social networking help keep people connected to each other but both can also be a huge distraction.

agonizing over what pictures and facts to include, what activities to highlight, and how much personal information to reveal, while others readily admit to willfully distorting facts to make their online identity appear more interesting. At times, choosing how to portray oneself becomes a kind of performance. As Turkle writes, "On social networking sites such as Facebook, we think we will be presenting ourselves, but our profile ends up as somebody else—often the fantasy of who we want to be."[23]

Creating a profile can also feed adolescent insecurities. As one high school student commented:

> When you have to represent yourself on Facebook to convey to anyone who doesn't know you what and who you are, it leads to a kind of obsession about minute details about yourself. . . . I know for girls, trying to figure out, "Oh, is this picture too revealing to put? Is it prudish if I don't put it?" You have to think carefully for good reason, given how much people will look at your profile and obsess over it. You have to know that everything you put up will be perused very carefully. And that makes it necessary for you to obsess over what you do put up and how you portray yourself.[24]

Another high school senior comments that even her list of Facebook friends becomes part of her online persona. When asked to confirm someone as a friend on Facebook, she says, "I always feel a panic. . . . Who should I friend? . . . I really only want to have my cool friends listed, but I'm nice to a lot of other kids at school. So I include the more unpopular ones, but then I'm unhappy."[25]

Another way that young people manage their online identity is to constantly broadcast what they are doing from moment to moment. Some experts worry that this constant disclosure of private information and wrangling of online identity supplants authentic communication and may lead to self-centeredness and even narcissism, a personality disorder marked by a grandiose view of oneself.

Sharing Stories

Others contend that the constant postings about self merely fulfills an innate human urge to connect with others and pass on information—an ancient process that is just accelerated online. As Cohen says,

> We share stories. We're designed to. If something surprises, delights, or disgusts us, we feel an innate urge to pass it on. The same impulse that makes Internet videos "go viral" has been spreading ideas (and jokes, and chain letters) throughout history. . . . And of course we're telling our own stories, too. We read regularly about celebrity bloggers with millions of fans, or Twitter campaigns that influence world events. But the truth is that most bloggers, vloggers, tweeters, and Facebookers are talking mainly to their friends. They compare lunches, swap songs, and share the small stories of their day. They're not trying to be novelists or *The New York Times*. They're just reclaiming their place at the center of their lives.[26]

To what extent today's new arena for self-expression will forge social ties and shape interpersonal communication is unknown. What is certain is that people will continue to use social networking tools to reinforce established friendships, forge new relationships, and stay in touch with the latest happenings.

Facts

- In a British study, three-quarters of college students surveyed said that Facebook played an important role in helping them adjust to college life.

- The fastest growing demographic of social network users are people aged 35 and older.

- A 2010 study by the Mental Health Foundation reported that 31 percent of respondents aged 18–34 felt they spent too much time interacting online.

CHAPTER THREE

How Has Social Networking Impacted Political and International Events?

S ocial networking's impact on world events has been and continues to be profound. As Clay Shirky explained in a 2010 TED Talk:

> Media, the media landscape that we knew, as familiar as it was, as easy conceptually as it was to deal with the idea that professionals broadcast messages to amateurs, is increasingly slipping away. In a world where media is global, social, ubiquitous and cheap, in a world of media where the former audience is in that world, media is less and less often about crafting a single message to be consumed by individuals. It is more and more often a way of creating an environment for convening and supporting groups.[27]

In this way, social networking has empowered individuals and groups to influence world events. As Sascha Segan notes in *PC*

Magazine, "Connected people are empowered people. If we consider democracy to be a priority in the U.S., we have to make connectivity a priority too."[28] Social networking's impact on information sources has been slowly but inexorably becoming a part of how the world gets its news. As journalist Jose Antonio Vargas writes,

Think of Google, which in a span of 12 years has become synonymous with and inseparable from the Internet; of Wikipedia, the write-it yourself encyclopedia. . . . Think of YouTube, home of a plethora of user-generated videos, where a madman and a freedom fighter can carve out his or her own space; and Twitter, . . . arguably the most effective broadcast channel in the world, giving voice to anyone, anywhere, with a mobile or Internet connection. This ongoing shift is still very much in its infancy.[29]

When everyone can participate in every issue by being able to express an opinion, post a YouTube video, or research a political candidate or issue, many aspects of government are more transparent. Some see this type of transparency as a good thing. Mark Zuckerberg notes in *The Facebook Effect*, "A more transparent world creates a better-governed world and a fairer world."[30] Zuckerberg and others view the democratization of information as an incredible gift to humanity. Former State Department employee Jared Cohen claims, "I call this digital democracy. Facebook is one of the most organic tools for democracy promotion the world has ever seen."[31]

Though many agree with this assessment, governments worldwide are adjusting to this new transparency with varying degrees of cooperation. Even the world's leader in democracy, the United States, has felt the sting of the new information technologies. In 2011, when WikiLeaks founder Julian Assange leaked secret papers about the war in Iraq—specifically about hidden Iraqi civilian casualty numbers, the impossibility of training the Iraqi army to take over in Iraq, and other news not previously made public—President Barack Obama and the Defense Department were incensed. New

"Connected people are empowered people. If we consider democracy to be a priority in the U.S., we have to make connectivity a priority too."[28]

— Sascha Segan, journalist and lead analyst for PCMag Mobile.

Social Media Missteps on the Campaign Trail

In 2011 a quirky campaign ad for presidential hopeful Herman Cain served as a dramatic example of how politicians are using YouTube and other social media tools to get their message out. Cain began as an almost unknown Republican candidate. Yet his well-publicized position on taxes gained him a loyal, if small, following.

Cain tried to use the fact that he was a Washington outsider who would go directly to the public to appeal to voters. Yet his lack of the use of traditional hand-holders and image makers became apparent when he released a video on YouTube in support of his candidacy. In the low-budget video, his campaign manager, Mark Block, claims that Cain's candidacy is groundbreaking in many ways. He ends the video by lighting a cigarette and smoking it on camera. In the next cut, Herman Cain is shown taking an excruciatingly long seven seconds to break into a smile. The video was released on Twitter and Facebook and quickly became a sensation as it was brutally mocked and generated dozens of parodies, including parodies by television comedians Jon Stewart and Stephen Colbert.

Cain ultimately dropped his presidential bid, although for reasons unrelated to the video. However, the ad seemed to show that using social media to directly engage the public can go terribly wrong.

York representative Peter King, chairman of the House Homeland Security Committee, claimed that Assange's leaks were as dangerous as a military attack on the United States and called for WikiLeaks to be labeled a terrorist organization.

The federal government quickly moved to prosecute Assange. Some in the United States even called for his execution. Clearly, the type of transparency that is now available via the Internet, where one man can instantly release information to the world, is challenging government secrecy.

Aiding World Revolutions?

Putting the proverbial genie back in the bottle, however, is no longer possible. The effects of social networking technologies are making revolution more feasible. Early on, the world saw how these new social networking methods could be used to successfully foment revolution on a large scale. In 2001, for example, texting enabled Filipinos to gather in large numbers to protest and eventually oust their political leader.

In 2009 Iranian citizens also resorted to social media to publicize and organize protests. When Mahmoud Ahmadinejad was declared the winner over Mir-Hossein Mousavi in Iran's presidential election, accusations of vote tampering and polling abnormalities brought those results into question. Massive protests erupted, and the government promptly shut down traditional media sources in an attempt to control information about the protests. However, Twitter, Facebook, Flickr, and YouTube took the place of these media outlets to release information on the dissent. Even the US government understood the importance of these sites, discussing and coordinating with Twitter to reschedule regular site maintenance and remain online so that this vital news outlet would be available for citizens' real-time updates.

Unlike in the Philippines, however, Iran's social media revolution did not result in a massive change. However, many commentators believe that it did allow for a shift in citizen participation and power. The Iranian government could not crack down on its citizens the way it had in the past, with the entire world watching its every move. Others are more doubtful that Iran's elections represented a "Twitter Revolution." Gaurav Mishra, cofounder of media analysis company 20:20 WebTech, contends, "I think the idea of a Twitter revolution is very suspect. The amount of people who use these tools in Iran is very small and could not support protests that size."[32]

Ethan Zuckerman, a senior researcher at Harvard University's

Berkman Center for Internet & Society, agrees. "Social media are helpful in exposing what's happening to the outside world, but it's a mistake to think that these protests [in Iran] are because of social media. It's more conventional things like word-of-mouth and phone calls that really bring massive numbers of people into the streets."[33]

A Major Conduit

Yet revolution continues throughout the Middle East, and social media seem to be a major conduit to keep it going. In Egypt in 2011, citizen protests, along with the support of the military, ousted long-time dictator Hosni Mubarek. One of the key figures in the protests, Wael Ghonim, directly credits Facebook with his and other protesters' ability to keep the revolutionary movement going and to keep it in the public eye:

> I want to meet Mark Zuckerberg one day and thank him . . . I'm talking on behalf of Egypt. . . . This revolution

A jubilant young Libyan in Tripoli in 2011 celebrates his country's liberation after learning of the death of dictator Mu'ammar Gadhafi. News of Gadhafi's death spread quickly as Libyans posted photos of his corpse on YouTube and Facebook.

started online. This revolution started on Facebook. This revolution started . . . in June 2010 when hundreds of thousands of Egyptians started collaborating content. We would post a video on Facebook that would be shared by 60,000 people on their walls within a few hours. I've always said that if you want to liberate a society just give them the Internet.[34]

Malcolm Gladwell, a writer for the *New Yorker*, is incensed by the focus on social media rather than the root cause of revolution. He contends it takes away from the meaning of such revolutions. These revolutions are rooted in decades of injustice, and whether social media is used to foment them is the least important factor.

Surely the least interesting fact about [the revolutions] is that some of the protesters may (or may not) have at one point or another employed some of the tools of the new media to communicate with one another. Please. People protested and brought down governments before Facebook was invented. They did it before the internet came along. . . . People with a grievance will always find ways to communicate with each other. How they choose to do it is less interesting, in the end, than why they were driven to do it in the first place.[35]

Though the underlying roots of injustice and corruption are the primary factors in making citizens come together to overthrow unjust regimes, social networking has aided such efforts and made them far less easy for the world to ignore.

Transforming Society

While people debate the role of social media in countries currently undergoing political change, others are more concerned with the aftermath of that change. Some wonder whether social media can play a role in the governmental, political, and economic transformation of nations. Egypt and Iran, for example, have yet to replace their dictatorships with more freedom-loving regimes. Although initially supportive, Egypt's military, for example, seemed less interested in sharing the power after Mubarek's ouster. During elections in November 2011, the moderate Islamist Party won the election, but many radical Islamists were elected to the parliament. What this means for Egypt's future remains uncertain. It clearly is not moving toward a more democratic society since the ultraconservative Islamists neither believe in freedom for women nor in access to Western technologies and entertainment. Thus, whether social media is really a factor in ousting repressive regimes *and* initiating real change is still an open question.

In *The Net Delusion,* writer and academic Evgeny Morozov speculates that social media can do little to encourage democracy in lands that have long been subjected to political repression.

> Even if we assume that the Internet may facilitate the toppling of authoritarian regimes, it does not necessarily follow that it would also facilitate the consolidation of democracy. If anything, the fact that various antidemocratic forces—including extremists, nationalists, and former elites—have suddenly gained a new platform to mobilize and spread their gospel suggests that the consolidation of democracy may become harder rather than easier.[36]

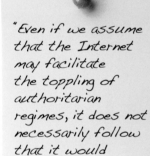

"Even if we assume that the Internet may facilitate the toppling of authoritarian regimes, it does not necessarily follow that it would also facilitate the consolidation of democracy."[36]

— Evgeny Morozov, author of *The Net Delusion.*

Morozov contends that because it is such an indiscriminate outlet, social media may be its own worst enemy, eventually making the general public turn against it and support government crackdowns on its use. Morozov goes on to say that in instances where "child pornographers, criminal gangs, nationalists, and terrorists use the Internet to cause more harm, the public's patience will sooner or later run out."[37] Even more dangerously, Morozov predicts, already unstable governments will not be able to control the populace, and undesirable opportunists may take advantage of power vacuums to initiate less personal freedom. "Multiply the power of the Internet by the incompetence of a weakened state, and what you get is a lot of anarchy and injustice. The reason why so many otherwise astute observers see democracy where there is none is that they confuse the democratization of access to tools with the democratization of society,"[38] Morozov concludes.

Eerily, some of Morozov's predictions seemed to be echoed in Libya. During uprisings against the government in Tunisia, Mu'ammar Gadhafi mocked protesters there for claiming that the Internet was a useful tool. His views were widely published on the Internet. It seemed ironic that a figure of repressive government would use the Internet to mock those talking about the influence of the Internet. Yet, only a few months later, a violent uprising in Libya would end in Gadhafi's capture and death at the hands of his own citizens, who immediately photographed pictures of Gadhafi's dead body and posted them to YouTube and Facebbook. Both incidents seem to reflect Morozov's worries. In the vacuum left by Gadhafi's violent and repressive reign, which ended in chaos, what form of government is likely to take its place? Many of these questions must be left to the future, as social media's impact leaves more questions than answers.

Domestic Politics

Within the United States, social media is already playing an influential part in politics. Many credit Obama's savvy use of the Internet with allowing him to harness so much of the youth vote during the 2008 presidential election. Online organizer for the Obama campaign Chris Hugh pioneered interactive sites for politicians. He created the site my.barackobama.com that allowed Obama supporters to organize, share information, and create places for rallies and fund-raisers. Even after the election, Hugh has gotten the president's message out via Twitter, Facebook, and other social media outlets. In addition, Obama himself has used Twitter to speak directly to his constituency on matters such as education and debt relief, for example.

With this success, every candidate is vying for an online presence in gearing up for the 2012 elections. Some believe that these new tactics especially appeal to voters under the age of 30, and prove that young voters will reenter the polls with new vigor. Calling young people the Net Gen, author Don Tapscott argues in

"People no longer have to follow leaders and do what they're told. Now they can organize themselves, publish themselves, and inform themselves."[39]

— Don Tapscott, author of *Grown Up Digital.*

Grown Up Digital that "in 2004, more people under the age of 30 cast votes than did people over 65. . . . In the 2008 primaries, young people flocked to the polls. . . . The Net Geners possess a tool of unprecedented power and are driving changes that could topple many established orders. . . . People no longer have to follow leaders and do what they're told. Now they can organize themselves, publish themselves, and inform themselves."[39] Tapscott and others believe that far from feeling alienated from politics, Net Geners believe that they no longer have to go through traditional institutions to create change; they can do it themselves.

The 2008 and 2012 campaigns of Ron Paul relied almost entirely on the Internet. Paul's mixed libertarian and Republican stances appealed to an unprecedented number of young people, many of whom had never encountered traditionally libertarian views of reinstating the gold standard or eliminating the IRS. Paul's campaign led many to speculate that the Internet may forge a new path for a viable third-party candidate. With candidates capable of engaging voters directly, the need for huge campaign financing, expensive advertisements, and currying favors may one day be unnecessary.

Online Campaigning Goes Mainstream

In a 2011 article in the online news site Mashable, reporter Alex Fitzpatrick states that online campaigning has become completely mainstream. He notes that online campaigning can work in three ways: first, by sharing ideals and experiences; second, by engaging followers; and third, by enlisting volunteers and other kinds of help. Fitzpatrick notes that some campaigns have begun to post video about the day-to-day events in the campaign office. Such videos can create an intimacy with voters that orating in front of a group cannot. In addition, online campaigning can enlist volunteers in local areas where a candidate is going to speak or meet with constituents. Such volunteers can aid in spreading the word about the candidate's event.

President Barack Obama, always eager to find ways to connect to voters, continues to capitalize on his online presence. On January 30, 2012, Obama provided an online video chat room to answer voters' questions about his State of the Union address.

By using social networking tools to directly engage the public, Obama hopes to create a new intimacy with voters. As part of Google's social networking site Google+, the company provided the president with the video chat room called "the Hangout," for 45 minutes. The chat room capped off a week of special social media engagements that the president planned around the State

The Death of Mu'ammar Gadhafi

In October 2011 videos posted on YouTube confirmed the bloody final moments of Libyan dictator Mu'ammar Gadhafi. A revolution to overthrow the dictator had begun on the heels of similar events in Tunisia, Iran, and Egypt. Gadhafi went into hiding after British airstrikes targeted his compound. The video of Gadhafi's final moments illustrates the confusing way pivotal world events are revealed when ordinary citizens post videos in real time.

Libya's deposed leader was hiding in a drain under a motorway in Sirte with a group of bodyguards when he was discovered and pulled from the drain. In a clutch of videos on the Internet he is seen begging his captors for mercy. The footage shows him incoherent and drenched in blood.

Wounded and terrified, Gadhafi appears deluded to the end, asking his captors: "What did I do to you?" It is clear that he is about to be killed. The videos left international media outlets searching for a context: By whom and how was Gaddafi killed? The actual answers remained elusive as various reporters tried to gain more information about the dictator's death. The videos echo the concerns voiced by author Evgeny Morozov in *The Net Delusion* that when social media propels events, the results can be violent and disturbing.

Quoted in Peter Beaumont and Chris Stephen, "Gaddafi's Last Words as He Begged for Mercy: 'What Did I Do to You?'" *Guardian*, October 22, 2011. www.guardian.co.uk.

of the Union speech. Google+ solicited questions over the video sharing site You Tube and asked users to vote on their favorites. The president answered these questions and spoke directly with a group delivering live questions.

New Grassroots Movements

While presidents and politicians use social networking to expand their reach and create connections with their constituencies, every day citizens are starting grassroots movements with the same networking tools. The conservative Tea Party began with a housewife's outrage at politics as usual. Blogger Beth Martin complained about politics. The blog gained traction, and, along with friend Amy Kremer, the two women were able to take the general outrage felt over the Obama bailout of banks during the economic crisis of 2010 and form it into a national organization. Today the Tea Party continues to make inroads, supporting fiscally conservative candidates and organizing protests.

Politicians who do not understand the new transparency created by the Internet may be doomed by their ignorance. In 2011 New York representative Anthony Weiner paid for his lack of Internet savvy by being forced to resign. Weiner sent compromising photos of himself to several women who followed him on Twitter. When these texts went public, Weiner claimed that his Internet account had been hacked—a virtual call to arms for every hacker and journalist to prove Weiner had sent the messages himself. When it was proved that only Weiner himself could have sent the messages, Weiner issued a public apology. Weiner went from a popular and influential political figure to a groveling and ashamed man within a week. Again, social networking had allowed for instant transparency. No longer is it possible for politicians and governments to simply deny their transgressions. While clearly, in Weiner's case, the Internet was used to expose hypocrisy, it has also been used as a tool to enhance the public good.

"By sharing images, texting, and tweeting, the public is already becoming part of a large response network, rather than remaining mere bystanders or casualties."[41]

— ScienceDaily, online science news website.

Disaster Relief

"Please can someone find some help for my friend 2 children that are alive under their house at 4813 Ruelle Chretien Lalu et Poupla Haiti."[40] In January 2009 this stark message was posted to a texting service used to summon emergency relief in areas, such as Haiti, hit with natural disasters. The texting service, using code 4636, allowed people to text emergency services for help with trapped people, fires, and requests for food, water, and medical supplies. Volunteers translated the messages from Creole and French into English, gave the location of the person sending the text, and then passed the messages on to American and English emergency services. Since many poor people in Third World countries have cell phones and use texting regularly, such sites have proved invaluable to relief organizations such as the Red Cross to pinpoint where their help is needed most. In addition, volunteers are given GPS mapping applications to locate areas that may be unfamiliar to rescuers. As ScienceDaily explains, "By sharing images, texting, and

Haitians line up for free medical care in the aftermath of a devastating 2010 earthquake that killed and injured many thousands of people. Relief agencies, attempting to provide food, water, and medical supplies, located people in need with the help of cell phone texts and tweets.

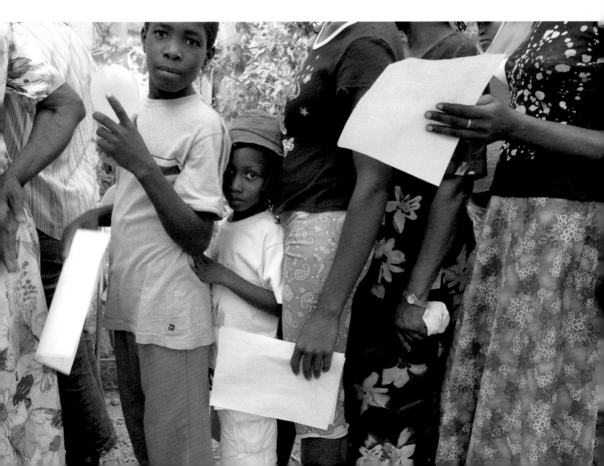

tweeting, the public is already becoming part of a large response network, rather than remaining mere bystanders or casualties."[41]

Social networks allow people recovering from disaster to connect immediately with emergency services. During the 2009 H1N1 influenza pandemic, the US Department of Health and Human Services' "Mommycast" over YouTube gave over 1 million viewers information about the disease, including how the flu spread and where to get vaccinations. Many public health officials believe this is only the beginning of what could become the most effective tool yet to keep people informed about public health. According to journalist Charlotte Tucker, "As technology has advanced, so too have the ways that public health officials are communicating with the public. Twitter, Facebook, and smartphone apps have become the latest tools in the public health and disaster preparedness fields, in part because they allow officials to reach a large number of people quickly with important information."[42]

Perhaps the best use of the Internet, particularly sites like Twitter, are the real-time updates that help keep information flowing not only to the outside world but among friends and family separated by natural disasters. During the 2011 earthquake in Japan, Twitter and Facebook became favored ways to communicate when phone lines were overwhelmed. "Twitter played a great role in the first few days after the quake,"[43] says Japanese tech journalist Nobuyuki Hayashi. One Japanese city started a Twitter account to inform residents when the power company had scheduled blackouts. Other cities followed suit, quickly forming their own Twitter presence to update information.

On both the international and domestic fronts, the Internet is changing the way the world communicates. Just how this communication will have a real impact on world governments, however, remains to be seen.

Facts

- According to a 2011 Pew Internet survey, 73 percent of adult Internet users went online to get news about the 2010 midterm elections.

- According to an American Red Cross survey, more than 30 percent of people would turn to social media to let their loved ones know they are safe in the event of a national disaster.

- In the aftermath of the 2010 earthquake in Haiti, a charity text message campaign raised more than $10 million for Haiti victim relief.

- Only one-quarter of the Egyptian populace has access to online sources.

- The world first learned of Mu'ammar Gadhafi's death via an e-mail from the information center of the Misrata military council on October 20, 2011.

CHAPTER FOUR

How Does Social Networking Affect Education and the Workplace?

One of the central pillars of education and learning is the ability to focus. Not surprisingly, social networking—and the Internet era in general—is radically changing the way people pay attention and learn. Educators worry that many young people today are less attentive than previous generations. They believe that young people are bombarded with a stream of rapidly changing information that may be eroding their attention span and ability to think deeply. Whether these concerns will lead to a reshaping of traditional models of education is the subject of much debate.

Scattered Attention

Cellphones, iPods, and computers have become a central feature in classrooms throughout the world. In a widely read article titled "Is Google Making Us Stupid?" Nicholas Carr discusses the effect of Internet distraction on learning—and overall cognition in general. Carr makes the case that the access to so much information is distracting and leads to skimming, browsing, and fragmented thinking as opposed to deep and probing thought. As Carr writes, "What the Net seems to be doing is chipping away my capacity for concentration and contemplation. My mind now expects to take in information the way the Net distributes it: in a swiftly moving stream of particles."[44]

Carr describes why using networked computers in the school setting—a common practice in many educational settings today—may have a particularly negative effect on students and others:

> The experience of reading words on a networked computer, whether it's a PC, an iPhone, or a Kindle, is very different from the experience of reading those same words in a book. As a technology, a book focuses our attention, isolates us from the myriad distractions that fill our everyday lives. A networked computer does precisely the opposite. It is designed to scatter our attention. It doesn't shield us from environmental distractions; it adds to them. The words on a computer screen exist in a welter of contending stimuli."[45]

Laptops, tablets, e-readers, and cell phones have become essential tools in schools and classrooms worldwide. Some experts worry that students do so much online skimming and browsing using tools like these that they are losing the ability to concentrate and think more deeply.

Sherry Turkle concurs that today's students, who are bombarded by multiple sources of information competing for their attention, are increasingly showing an attention span in the classroom akin to their attention span on Facebook. She states that "online reading—at least for the high school and college students I have studied—always invites you elsewhere. And it is only sometimes interrupted by linking to reference works and associated commentaries. More often, it is broken up by messaging, shopping, Facebook, MySpace, and YouTube."[46]

The Lure of Instant Gratification

Today's students are always an arm's length away from a cell phone or computer, and many worry that these technologies provide instant gratification rather than promoting the patience required to read through multiple sources to glean information and come to an in-depth understanding or analysis. A number of scientific studies have confirmed that trying to navigate the glut of information available online degrades the ability to acquire knowledge. As far back as 1997, researcher Jakob Nielsen found that a full 79 percent of online readers merely scan content. Nielsen writes that online readers "want to decide what to read and how to read it, and resent being at the mercy of an omniscient author who will take them on a meandering, circuitous path, before delivering, maybe, the nugget of information they are after. Online readers want their nugget now, and will scan a couple of paragraphs quickly for it, then forever desert the page if the initial glance yields nothing promising."[47]

A study at the University of California at Los Angeles likewise confirmed that the constant switching from one page to another—and multitasking in general—chips away at a student's ability to learn. As Russell Poldrack, coauthor of the study, describes it: "Even if you learn while multitasking, that learning is less flexible and more specialized, so you cannot retrieve the information as easily. . . . When distractions force you to pay less attention to what you are

"What the Net seems to be doing is chipping away my capacity for concentration and contemplation. My mind now expects to take in information the way the Net distributes it: in a swiftly moving stream of particles."[44]

— Technology writer Nicholas Carr.

doing, you don't learn as well as if you had paid full attention."[48]

Don Tapscott, chairman of the nGeneration Innovation Network, disagrees that multitasking is bad for student's brains. In his book *Grown Up Digital*, Tapscott expresses the view that digital immersion and multitasking actually helps students. He writes that

> if they can learn to feed off of more sources of information in real time, while they are writing an essay or tackling a complicated problem, I think they're more productive than I was at their age, when I sat down with some textbooks and tried to make sense of them and come up with a novel idea. I think the kids have got it right. Allowing yourself to absorb new bits of information while you're working is not necessarily a distraction. Working this way certainly helps me to develop the capability to think profoundly. [49]

"*Students using social networking sites are actually practicing the kinds of 21st century skills we want them to develop to be successful today.*"[50]

— Christine Greenhow, educational researcher and research fellow at the Institute for Advanced Studies.

Skills for the Twenty-First Century

Like Tapscott, other educators and observers extol the benefits of social networking on the grounds that it will help students be successful in contemporary society. Since social networking is not going away, these proponents believe, digital tools should be integrated into the educational process because networked students not only have access to a wellspring of information on a diverse range of subjects and perspectives but also get valuable practice using cutting-edge technology.

Christine Greenhow, educational researcher and research fellow at the Institute for Advanced Studies says that her research confirms that learning to use these technologies benefits students:

> What we found is that students using social networking sites are actually practicing the kinds of 21st century skills we want them to develop to be successful today. Students are developing a positive attitude towards using technology systems, editing and customizing content and thinking about online design and layout. They're also sharing

creative original work like poetry and film and practicing safe and responsible use of information and technology. The Web sites offer tremendous educational potential.[50]

Tapscott concurs with Greenhow, adding that although students will clearly gain knowledge differently, with perhaps less depth, this will "fit the demands of . . . a world in which the ability to think and learn and find out things is more important than mastering a static body of knowledge."[51] Tapscott views the future world as one where a person's ability to succeed will depend on his or her ability to sift through ever-changing content.

Learning Beyond the Borders of the Classroom

Seeking novel approaches to educating their students, a number of teachers across the country are starting to integrate social networking technologies into their curriculum. Many of these educators focus on using social networking sites and tools to connect students from disparate parts of the world and foster cross-cultural communication. A teacher from Greece describes how her school cooperates with schools from countries such as the Netherlands, France, England, and Sweden to facilitate language learning. The schools use social networking tools so that students not only practice their language skills with other students but also share stories about their cultures and lives.

Silvia Rosenthal Tolisano is a twenty-first-century learning specialist who is also adopting social networking at her private kindergarten-through-eighth-grade school, Gottlieb Day School, in Jacksonville, Florida. Tolisano launched her project "Around the World with 80 Schools" in 2009. Using a social networking site, she invited teachers everywhere to participate, attracting 300 educators from across the globe. Using Skype, Tolisano's students communicate with students in Canada, Finland, New Zealand, and many other countries. When a group of students at Gottlieb Day School were learning about orca whales, for example, they talked to students

"These days people toss around the term 'addiction' as casually as they would a Frisbee. But whatever you call an unhealthy attachment, people are spending ever more time on social networks, and some are getting in trouble for it."[58]

— David DiSalvo, freelance writer.

in British Columbia, whose coastal waters are home to orcas. Soon after, the British Columbia students shot video footage of orcas, which they then forwarded to the students in Florida. In light of these experiences, Tolisano believes that social networking "creates global awareness that there is a wider world out there and that we are not alone. [Students] find that it is just as easy to collaborate with a class in England as with the class next door."[52]

Math teacher Mary Hosten is another educator using cutting-edge social networking technologies in her classroom. Hosten describes how she is using these tools to make mathematics meaningful to students. In her class, students post a joke online and then track how fast and far the joke spreads, based on how many times, and where, the joke is reposted. As Hosten says: "Social networking is an excellent real-world example of discrete mathematics. Students can post a joke and then track the vertex edge

With the help of social networking sites, an orca whale school project brought together Canadian students in British Columbia and American students in Florida. Many teachers are finding creative uses for social networking tools in their classrooms.

graph that results. The graph can be used to make inferences about popularity, outgoing personalities, and levels of friendship. Tracking the joke as a tree may also allow you to make inferences about natural communities, cliques."[53]

While it is unclear how far educators will go to adopt new strategies in the classroom, a student who is unfamiliar with new technologies will most likely be left behind. Yet fully embracing social media may also have undesirable consequences.

The Perils of Constant Connectivity

Never before have young people been so connected to one another. Some studies suggest that a whopping 92 percent of students socialize online. Researchers and parents worry that the copious amount of time spent twittering, texting, and checking statuses and profiles will take precedence over homework and other academic pursuits. A 2010 study by the Kaiser Family Foundation appears to lend some credence to these concerns, reporting that students aged 8 to 18 years old who spend the most time on social media have lower grades and even lower levels of personal contentment. A study published in *Computers in Human Behavior* in 2011 reported that time spent on Facebook was negatively related to overall GPA.

Yet it seems unlikely that students will give up their devices any time soon. Turkle describes social media's huge appeal: "Our neurochemical response to every ping and ring tone seems to be the one elicited by the "seeking" drive, a deep motivation of the human psyche. Connectivity becomes a craving; when we receive a text or an e-mail, our nervous system responds by giving us a shot of dopamine. We are stimulated by connectivity itself. We learn to require it, even as it depletes us."[54] Turkle and others believe that students who use social networking are not unlike Pavlov's dogs, who salivated every time they heard a stimulus (such as a bell) that signaled they were about to be fed. The instant gratification of communication signaled by a ping or ring tone draws one's immediate curiosity to find out who is sending the information. In a sense, students are becoming slaves to their connectivity, where the stimulus becomes the most fulfilling thing in their lives.

A 2011 study appears to support the premise that the lure of

Roommate's Fun Leads to Suicide

Eighteen-year-old Rutgers University freshman Tyler Clementi was an accomplished violinist who had received a college scholarship from the Ridgewood Symphony Orchestra. Clementi was a shy student who preferred to keep the fact that he was gay private.

That was until his roommate Dharun Ravi, 18, and an accomplice, set up a camera in Clementi's dorm room and used it to view Clementi having a sexual encounter with another male. The two wrote about the encounter on a live Twitter feed.

When Clementi learned of his public humiliation, he simply could not face his life. He killed himself by jumping off the George Washington Bridge. The incident shocked parents and students at Rutgers. In March 2012 a New Jersey jury found Ravi guilty of invasion of privacy, bias intimidation (which is a hate crime), and other charges.

social networking is so strong because it taps into a deep-seated human need to be connected to others. Researcher Martin Lindstrom set out to determine whether iPhones and BlackBerrys tap into the same pathways in the brain that make other behaviors—like gambling or overeating—irresistible and even addictive to some people. In the study, subjects were exposed to audio and video of a ringing and vibrating iPhone while their brain activity was monitored on an MRI. Strikingly, Lindstrom found a "flurry of activation in the insular cortex of the brain, which is associated with feelings of love and compassion. The subjects' brains responded to the sound of their phones as they would respond to the presence or proximity of a girlfriend, boyfriend, or family member. In short, the subjects didn't demonstrate the classic brain-based signs of addiction. Instead, they *loved* their iPhones."[55] Based on these findings, Lindstrom believes that the term "addiction" in relation to social media may not be scientifically accurate. Because of the unique way that social networking affects brain activity, moreover, many proponents believe that attempting to prohibit the use of social media in schools and other venues would be futile.

Cyberbullying

In addition to the potential problems related to constant connectivity, social networking can also foster troubling behavior for certain students who lack interpersonal skills and as such prefer the online world to the offline world. For these individuals the near constant use of social networking may further erode social skills and real-world relationships. It may also amplify peer aggression and harassment. Because social networking is generally bereft of social cues such as facial expressions, for example, it may be easier for a bully to harass, degrade, or threaten a person via a computer or cell phone. Using social networking to bully also ensures a certain anonymity—the bully no longer has to see the pained expression of his or her victim. In the past, moreover, victims could get away from schoolyard bullies when they headed home. Now, constant connectivity ensures bullies can torment their victims 24/7. Bullying victims, often lacking maturity, see the social disgrace of this constant harassment as too much to bear.

The extent of cyberbullying—and how it impacts learning and student well-being—is difficult to quantify. Some studies say approximately 30 percent of students have reported being the victim of some kind of bullying. According to recent research by Sameer Hinduja and Justin Patchin of the Cyber Bullying Research Center, victims of cyberbullying were almost twice as likely to have attempted suicide compared with youth who had not been cyberbullied.

Although kids have always been teased and taunted, cyberbullying allows for the taunting to be spread to a much wider audience. A mother describes how her autistic son, reluctant to go to a school dance, overcame his fears to attend and to venture out on the dance floor. A classmate secretly videotaped him, posting the boy's awkward dancing on the net for all of his classmates to see. "The level of cruelty was just astounding to me,"[56] said Representative Marty Walz, author of a Massachusetts antibullying law.

Anonymity and instant access to large numbers of people represent two of the downsides of the interconnected world of social media. John Halligan (pictured) displays a web page devoted to his adolescent son who killed himself after being relentlessly bullied, threatened, and taunted online.

Social Media in the Workplace

While schools grapple with how to curb cyberbullying and regain control of focus in the classroom by placing limits on social media, businesses are also facing issues related to these new technologies. Unlike the school environment, businesses have lagged behind in the desire to integrate social media into their employees' days. Many employers severely limit or completely restrict employees' use of the Internet, and most explicitly ban checking Facebook or other online message sites during work time. Many employers use spyware to check up on time spent on the Internet and what sites are being accessed by employees, to keep track of lost productivity.

As younger people are joining the workforce, however, many question these prohibitions, often proving to their employer that such tools allow them to improve their mental focus and their ability to network with fellow employees.

Jeanne C. Meister and Karie Willyerd are cofounders of Future Workplace and the authors of the book *The 2020 Workplace: How Innovative Companies Attract, Develop, and Keep Tomorrow's Employees Today.* Meister and Willyerd believe that social media tools such as Twitter, blogs, and social networks are beneficial in that they facilitate communication and foster collaboration and creative approaches to problem solving. They write that "more companies are discovering that an uber-connected workplace is not just about implementing a new set of tools—it is also about embracing a cultural shift to create an open environment where employees are encouraged to share, innovate and collaborate virtually."[57]

Despite such positive affirmations, lost productivity continues to be an issue for employers, with employees surfing the web, checking e-mails, and switching to check updates on networking sites. Some employees have a difficult time avoiding checking sites like Facebook, keeping the page open while they work at their computers and constantly checking it for new posts while adding posts of their own. According to David DiSalvo, writing in *Scientific American Mind*: "These days people toss around the term 'addiction' as casually as they would a Frisbee. But whatever you call an unhealthy attachment, people are spending ever more time on social networks, and some are getting in trouble for it."[58]

Even people who are motivated to stay on task find it difficult to ignore the lure of their e-mail ping as they work. As one professor of economics writes: "I'm trying to write. My article is due. But I'm checking my e-mail every two minutes. And then, the worst is when I change the setting so that I don't have to check the e-mail. It just comes in with a 'ping.' So now I'm like Pavlov's dog. I'm sitting around, waiting for the ping. I should ignore it. But I go right to it."[59]

"I suppose I do my job better, but my job is my whole life. . . . I am on my BlackBerry until two in the morning. I don't sleep well, but I still can't keep up with what is sent to me."[62]

— Diane, a museum curator.

Effect on Productivity

With so many media reports of social networking technologies leading to compulsive behaviors that interfere with work and productivity, scientists have started to scrutinize the nature and scope of the problem. A study by Nucleus Research in Boston found that some users of Facebook and other social networking technologies are spending two hours a day on the site while they are at work. Some experts estimate that this costs companies whose employees use Facebook at work 1.5 percent of total office productivity.

At the same time, other studies seem to suggest that social

Networking with Colleagues

Many educators are starting to use social networking systems to share their expertise with teachers from across the globe. Educator Jan MacNamara from Queensland, Australia, describes how she and her colleagues have harnessed the power of social networks to develop professionally:

> The power of the Personal Learning Network that our staff taps into would be impossible without the global interactions and connections our teachers have made through social networking tools. We . . . have established valuable networks for our teaching teams. In a recent Modern Foreign Language Teachers' workshop, one of our team sent out a tweet inviting practitioners to share their expertise. We were amazed at the response we received, and without so much as a blink of the eye—we switched into Skype mode and there was a 'new' face in our workshop—sharing their ideas and success stories from the U.K.

Quoted in Meris Stansbury, "Ten Ways Schools Are Using Social Media Effectively," *eSchool News*, October 21, 2011. www.eschoolnews.com.

networking actually boosts productivity in the workplace. Some researchers report that the tendency for the mind to wander off task and seek a break is normal—and not that terrible. An article in *ComputerWorld UK* cites evidence found in a 2011 study by Australian scientists, who collected data on 20,000 people using the Internet and social media in the workplace. The study found that using social media during office hours actually increased productivity by 9 percent, "whether it's checking out a funny video recommended by a Facebook friend or reading an interesting blog post tweeted by one of your followers, social media offers a brief escape that can replenish a workers' energy and give their mind a rest before they return to the rigours of the job."[60] In fact, such breaks may increase productivity simply because a worker does not have to leave his or her desk to walk down the hall to talk to a coworker, ending up in a lengthy conversation.

One member of the Australian research team, Rajesh Vasa, is a software engineer and lecturer at Swinburne University of Technology's Faculty of Information & Communication Technologies. According to Vasa, over 80 percent of social media used in the workplace is of a personal nature. He claims, however, that "when [employees] use social media, they do it in short bursts. A good way to think of it is like looking out the window for a short while to refresh your eyes. . . . We can say that the usage in the majority of cases is not high enough to be a serious distraction to normal work duties."[61]

> "The days of you having a different image for your work friends or co-workers and for the other people you know are probably coming to an end pretty quickly."[64]
>
> — Mark Zuckerberg, Facebook founder.

The Need for Speed

Employers who see a positive side to networking and Internet use, however, often do not see the workday ending at 5 p.m. Many employers expect employees to be continually online and available. Some employers expect employees to check in and answer e-mails while on vacation, to be available for online meetings in the evenings, and to accept text and e-mails at all hours. According to Diane, a curator at a large museum in the Midwest, "I suppose I do my job better, but my job is my whole life. Or my whole life is my job. When I move from calendar, to address book, to e-mail, to text messages, I feel like a master of the universe; everything is so efficient. I am a maximizing machine. I am on my BlackBerry until two in the morning. I don't sleep well, but I still can't keep up with what is sent to me."[62]

Clients, too, expect vendors to be available whenever they are, and to complete work on ever-changing, and often tighter, schedules. One Boston attorney named Trey describes legal matters that call for "time and nuance," but continues that "people don't have patience for these now. They send an e-mail, and they expect something back fast. They are willing to forgo the nuance; really, the client wants to hear something now." Trey concludes that electronic communication "has put me on a speed-up, on a treadmill, but that isn't the same as being productive." [63]

High Visibility

With the use of the Internet and especially sites such as the professional online networking site LinkedIn, it is growing increasingly difficult to have a personal life that remains unknown to one's employer. As Mark Zuckerberg notes, "The days of you having a different image for your work friends or co-workers and for the other people you know are probably coming to an end pretty quickly . . . [and] having two identities for yourself is an example of a lack of integrity."[64] Prospective employers, for example, are not beyond going onto Facebook and checking up on an applicant's private habits. And what employees post in the privacy of their own homes can also be subject to on-the-job scrutiny. For example, a Los Angeles web designer and graphic artist who made her workplace and coworkers a subject of her personal, home-based online blog was fired as a result of her posts. After her firing, she realized that she had blurred the lines of professional conduct.

Social networking continues to blur the line between personal and private life. In the years ahead, the traditional roles of teacher and student, and employee and employer, will continue to be adjusted and redefined.

Facts

- According to a 2011 harmon.ie survey of 515 employees, nearly 60 percent of work interruptions involve e-mail, text messaging, social networks, and other social media tools.

- A study at the University of New Hampshire found no correlation between amount of time spent on Facebook and student grades.

- A study released by Ohio State University shows that college students who use Facebook spend less time studying and have lower grades than those who do not.

- According to a study of 2,500 employees by AT&T, 65 percent said that social networking made their colleagues and themselves more efficient at work.

- According to a Ball State University study, most Americans spend at least 8.5 hours a day looking at screens—a television, computer monitor, or mobile phone.

- Australian scientists at the University of Melbourne concluded that the mental relief provided to workers from judicious use of social media sites, blogs, and YouTube during office hours increased productivity by 9 percent.

CHAPTER FIVE

Does Social Networking Pose a Threat to Privacy?

The number of people sharing copious amounts of personal information on social networking sites is soaring. As people are becoming more comfortable divulging information about their friendships, interests, and personal history, their lives may become increasingly transparent, with full details about their off-line lives available for many people to peruse. This so-called radical transparency, as Facebook founder Mark Zuckerberg calls it, may be fostering new norms about how society views private behavior. How to deal with this growing visibility—and the new privacy norms it engenders—are questions at the center of the social networking debate.

New Attitudes About Privacy

It appears that traditional notions of privacy may soon be obsolete. In 2006, for example, Facebook launched its "News Feed," a feature that actively broadcasts updates on a user's page to every one of his or her contacts. Immediately, there was a flood of complaints by users who did not want to give every friend unfettered access to so much personal information. As journalist Clive Thompson reported in the *New York Times*:

Just about every little thing you changed on your page was now instantly blasted out to hundreds of friends, including potentially mortifying bits of news—Tim and Lisa broke up; Persaud is no longer friends with Matthew—and drunken photos someone snapped, then uploaded and tagged with names . . . it was now like being at a giant, open party filled with everyone you know, able to eavesdrop on what everyone else was saying, all the time.[65]

After the initial panic subsided, however, Facebook enjoyed a huge boom in membership as users quickly became accustomed to having intimate details about their social world readily available for all to see. Today, news feed features are a pillar of social networking, and it appears that many users—especially young people—operate online with little expectation of privacy.

Evolutionary biologist Seirian Sumner contends this may be

Many of today's young adults and teens view privacy differently than previous generations. They seem willing to reveal a great deal about themselves online, including posting celebratory and somewhat compromising photos such as this one for all to see.

because users are more willing to tolerate invasions of privacy when they occur online. As Sumner relates:

> Caution and suspicion of the unfamiliar are ancestral traits of humans, ensuring survival by protecting against usurpation and theft of resources. A peculiar thing about the Internet is that it makes us highly receptive and indiscriminate in our interactions with complete strangers. The other day I received a message inviting me to join a Facebook group for people sharing "Seirian" as their first name. Can I resist? Of course not! . . . If the Facebook Seirians had knocked on my real front door instead of my virtual one, would I have signed up? No, of course not—too invasive, personal, and potentially costly. . . . Contrary to our ancestral behaviors, we tolerate invasion of privacy online.[66]

Some observers argue that these changing norms—and the new world of radical transparency—will create a more open, healthier society. For example, the world of social networking makes it increasingly difficult to support having different identities: In a business context, for example, users might reveal an identity separate from their personal or educational endeavors. In contrast, according to Zuckerberg, Facebook and other sites foster honesty and accountability by encouraging people to behave consistently and authentically. Zeynep Tufekci, a sociologist at the University of Maryland, studies how college students are adjusting to a world where everyone is watching. Tufekci shares Zuckerberg's view that the new awareness will encourage people to act with integrity, stating that "it's actually hard to lie because everybody knows the truth already. . . . You can't play with your identity if your audience is always checking up on you."[67]

Stephen Downes, a senior research officer of the National Research Council of Canada, believes that social networking sites and the transparency they foster will encourage not only honesty but also a deeper understanding of human nature—and human failings. This will ultimately create a more tolerant society in

"It's actually hard to lie because everybody knows the truth already. . . . You can't play with your identity if your audience is always checking up on you."[67]

— Zeynep Tufekci, a sociologist at the University of Maryland.

which it is accepted that people make mistakes or do embarrassing things, according to Downes, who argues that "it will be clear by 2020 that everybody has . . . skeletons (or nude photos or infidelities) in the closet, and it will be seen as absurd to make morality judgments based on these."[68] Michael Arrington of the technology blog *TechCrunch* also believes that the current generation will be less judgmental and hypocritical, writing that "we will simply become much more accepting of indiscretions over time. The point is, we don't really care about privacy anymore."[69]

Incessant Online Contact

That so many online users track virtually every single movement of their friends online creates other privacy issues as well. While the constant, up-to-the-minute updates of what people are doing may seem insignificant on their own, taken together over time these little bursts of information form a surprisingly accurate picture of other people's lives. Social scientists have started to use the term *ambient awareness* to describe the new type of awareness that develops from the incessant online contact with one's friends, family, acquaintances, and colleagues via social networking sites such as Facebook, MySpace, Twitter, Blogger, and others.

People have always been bombarded with tiny bits of mundane information in offline environments. These bits of information may seem so small or insignificant that most people do not notice them. However, just by being present, humans are processing these bits of information and making judgments based on them. In the physical world, for example, people pick up bits of information simply by being near someone and hearing snippets of conversation or watching body language. In the digital world, users are getting more information than ever, creating a heightened ambient awareness about everyday life.

Science and technology writer Clive Thompson describes how one avid user of social networking discovered that he could sense the rhythms of his friends' lives: "When one friend got sick with

"I don't care if you have taken every precaution to keep your information private to just a few people; all it takes is one friend copying and pasting that information and posting it somewhere else to 'breach' the privacy wall."[72]

— Ben Parr, technology journalist.

Identity Theft and Property Crime

Today, criminals can scour social networking sites and learn about users' personal whereabouts. In 2010 in New Hampshire, for example, a burglary ring targeted Facebook users who posted their locations; the group committed more than 50 break-ins when they knew the homeowners were on vacation or otherwise away from their homes.

A paper released in 2011 detailed a Canadian research study that showed how easy it is for criminals to infiltrate social networking sites. Researchers deployed 102 socialbots—programs designed to mimic real social media users—that sought out friend requests. The bots were so successful in securing friends that they were able to gain personal information from over 1 million users. Financial adviser Gail Buckner describes what can happen when strangers are given access to personal information intended for friends:

> ID thieves are mining the mother lode of personal information: social networking sites such as Facebook. These web sites are especially dangerous because users' guards are down, thinking the only people accessing their page are "friends." Often, someone will list juicy tidbits such as their birthday, the name of a parent or sibling, their home addresses . . . in other words the answers to some of the most common security questions you must respond to in order to gain access to websites containing extremely sensitive personal data—investment and financial accounts, government records, etc.

Gail Buckner, "How Thieves Use Facebook to Steal Your Identity," FoxBusiness, November 2, 2011. www.foxbusiness.com.

a virulent fever, he could tell by her Twitter updates when she was getting worse and the instant she finally turned the corner. He could see when friends were heading into hellish days at work or when they'd scored a big success. Even the daily catalog of sandwiches [that some users posted] became oddly mesmerizing, a sort of metronomic click that he grew accustomed to seeing pop up in the middle of the day."[70]

Too Much Information?

Ambient awareness is not only changing the nature of online privacy; it might also have a profound effect in the offline world. When people who are constantly in contact online do socialize face to face, they may feel more connected since they are already up to date on each other's movements. The downside is that when someone divulges information about what they are doing or where they will be, it is out there for all to see. Hence, a broad array of people may know, via the words and images posted on Facebook, MySpace, LinkedIn, Flickr, or other social media sites, details about a user's habits, daily routine, and personal whereabouts. Twitter even has a location function that allows users to attach their current location to their tweets. Similar functions have long been available on Facebook, too.

Many people worry that having their blow-by-blow activities and other pieces of information floating through cyber space. That and the development of location tracking could pose a threat to personal safety. If users tweet, for example, that they are going to the mall for an hour, that is an hour-long window during which their house could be robbed. One student at the University of Melbourne in Australia named Djana opines that the implications of location-based social networking "are either going to be, well . . . creepy, or just really, very annoying. That all of your 'friends' or 'followers' (most of whom you haven't seen in years and don't care to) can know where your local haunts are, where you live and what you do seems dangerous and unnecessary."[71]

> "Social media could become a means for total surveillance where the costs and impacts of today's breaches are a trifle by comparison."[78]
>
> — John Clippinger, codirector of the Law Lab at Harvard University.

Privacy Settings

Indeed, many people worry that the trend toward full disclosure is intrusive and excessive—and potentially damaging to private life. In response to these concerns, sites such as Facebook have added privacy settings so that users can adjust the default settings and limit how much of their personal information is shared. For example, users can discriminate among different kinds of friends and determine who sees what. Parents or relatives, consequently, could be prohibited from viewing fun party pictures. These privacy controls are highly underutilized, however. According to Facebook's chief privacy officer, only about 20 percent of Facebook members use the available privacy features. Others are simply unaware that privacy settings exist, or find them too troublesome to use.

Even if users are diligent in locking down everything with these tools, however, total privacy may still be elusive, because much of what is posted on social networking sites can be disseminated without permission: Photos, posts, and other snippets of information, which may disclose embarrassing, incriminating, or rash personal behavior, can be spread by another user almost instantly. Technology journalist Ben Parr writes:

> I don't care if you have taken every precaution to keep your information private to just a few people; all it takes is one friend copying and pasting that information and posting it somewhere else to "breach" the privacy wall. . . . An embarrassing picture can go from Facebook upload to public blog post in a matter of minutes. Even if you don't participate in any type of social media, someone can still take what they know about you and put it online.[72]

In his book *The Facebook Effect*, David Kirkpatrick recounts an incident that highlights the problem: "A young U.S. employee of Anglo-Irish Bank asked his boss for Friday off to attend to an unexpected family matter. Then someone posted a photo on Facebook of him at a party that same evening holding a wand and wearing a tutu. Everyone in the office—including his boss—discovered the lie."[73]

The Permanency of Social Networking

Compounding the debate is the fact that almost everything a user does online will be recorded for a lifetime, making it almost impossible to control privacy once something is broadcast to the world. One young man relates how he, as a college senior, had written a piece for the school newspaper about his use of craigslist to solicit sex with closeted gay men at Harvard University. The piece spread like wildfire in the online world. The man states that "it was a big hit," but goes on to say that "now, you know, three years later, I find that I'd really like to be an elementary school teacher. . . . It's really not something I want coming back to haunt me."[74] Ultimately, the man changed his name so that he would not be forever associated with his risqué behavior that is permanently cached online.

To many, such stories illustrate how inappropriate or embarrassing postings can do irreparable damage—and how easily someone can be unfairly judged on events that would have been unnoticed or quickly forgotten in the offline world. These critics worry that the unbridled disclosure of everything an individual has ever said or done may diminish the notion that people have a right to behave privately in the real world or that they can evolve over time as they learn from past experiences and adjust their behavior. Speaking to the permanency, high visibility, and other issues that pertain to social networking, President Barack Obama told a group of high school students in 2009, "I want everybody here to be careful about what you post on Facebook because in the YouTube age, whatever you do will be pulled up later somewhere in your life. And when you're young, you make mistakes and you do some stupid stuff."[75]

As users continue to grapple with how much personal information to disclose—and how to sequester that which they wish to remain private—Parr succinctly describes how he maintains his privacy, "What I want to keep private stays in my head."[76] This advice may have been especially prescient when Facebook experienced a technical problem in 2010 that resulted in a security lapse. At the time, a system error disabled the privacy settings on

The online world and the predominance of social media have raised various issues of concern. One of these issues is the way online data such as personal interests, buying habits, and more are bought and sold, often without the knowledge of the user.

the site's chat feature, which allows people to enjoy private conversations with their online friends. Consequently, many private messages were fully visible to unintended recipients. Although the situation was quickly resolved, this event illustrates the endless and unexpected ways that privacy can be breached in a world that operates largely online.

Consumer Protection Issues

Beyond ruined reputations or embarrassing revelations, there are many other consequences of having personal information widely accessible. One of the most vexing issues in the social networking debate is how users' online data is being bought and sold. The data, which is sold to advertisers as part of an enormous, multibillion-dollar industry, is collected in myriad ways. For example, companies use tracking software called cookies to identify and follow users as they move around the web. A company that identifies a business executive, for example, might sell that information to American Express, which then creates and delivers personalized ads to her.

Kathryn Montgomery writes in her book *Generation Digital* that digital technologies that enable marketers to delve into private behavior are not new: "Digital technologies make it possible to track every move, online and off, compiling elaborate personal profiles that combine behavioral, psychological, and social information on individuals."[77] The issue is much bigger today, however, because marketing companies can scour social networking sites and extract a substantial amount of information about consumers, including profile details and data on personal transactions, which can be used for marketing purposes. Because social networks encourage a torrent of sharing, they may be enabling outside sources to probe even more deeply into private lives. As journalist Joel Stein puts it, "From a [data] miner's point of view, Facebook has the most valuable trove of data ever assembled."[78]

Many users are simply unaware that companies are tapping into this data. One way that users lose control of this information is through the applications that MySpace, Facebook, and other sites allow outside users to create. One popular example is the photo sharing application that allows users to tag, or write a note about, a photo, and share it with friends. When users install these applications on their personal profile page, many do not realize that the application developers can see anything on the profile: a user's name, birthday, hometown, current location, and much more. According to Facebook's Platform Application Terms of Use, application makers can see "your political views, your activities, your interests, your musical preferences, television shows in which you are interested, movies in which you are interested, books in which you are interested . . . your education history, your work history, your course information" and many other facets of a user's personal life.[79]

Laws to Prohibit Sexual Predation and Cyberbullying

To date, there is no quick legal fix to protect children from cyberbullies, although online bullying and harassment via postings on social network sites represent a particularly offensive violation of personal privacy. High profile cases have brought the issue to the fore, however. In 2010 the case of Phoebe Prince of Massachusetts garnered widespread attention after the 15-year-old hanged herself after being bullied both at school and online; her tormentors even mocked her on Facebook following her death. Although most decry the relentless harassment that led to the teen's death, many feel that it is unnecessary to create new laws to prohibit behaviors, including bullying, that are already rendered illegal by existing laws. Nevertheless, five states toughened laws regarding online harassment following Prince's suicide.

Lawmakers similarly grapple with how best to crack down on sexual predators who may troll social networking sites to find victims, such as older men who lie about their age and identity so that they can seduce young girls into sending sexually explicit photos. According to Wired-Safety, there are roughly 6,000 reported cases of young people victimized by cyber-predators each year. Although most networking sites shut down profiles that feature pornographic images, many believe that new laws are needed to prevent the online sexual solicitation of children.

As John Clippinger, codirector of the Law Lab at Harvard University, puts it: "Social media could become a means for total surveillance where the costs and impacts of today's breaches are a trifle by comparison. Think medical information, DNA, all financial and commercial transactions, what you do, where you are and whom you talk to every minute of the day."[80] How this information could be used or misused has prompted many Internet scholars and other observers to call on lawmakers to take steps to control the massive flow of data.

Legislation

To date, no firmly established rules or regulations safeguard online privacy. Creating a uniform set of laws that address complex social issues like privacy is difficult, partly because privacy is a personal matter that means different things to different people. Some are very concerned with what they release online and how it is used, while others are completely indifferent. At the same time, experts differ on whether new laws should be crafted that specifically address the Internet or whether existing laws that protect privacy—whether online or in the real world—are adequate.

While there are no easy solutions, many call for strategies that would boost consumer awareness and empower users. To this end, a number of experts believe that it is primarily the responsibility of social networking sites to help their members understand and utilize available privacy settings. In this way, users who are concerned with privacy could control the amount of data that is bought and sold. Critics charge, however, that tight privacy settings limit not only consumer data, but also much of the social interactions that make these sites so appealing in the first place. Because they know that many users do not have the complex knowledge needed to activate the features that would protect privacy, some lawmakers call for regulations that would target the firms that collect data. As Senator John Kerry puts it: "Our privacy hangs in the balance every time we go online. You shouldn't have to be a computer genius to opt out of information sharing, but there are currently no comprehensive, baseline rules governing firms that collect information about us."[81]

"Facebook and other social technologies are increasingly important forums for public communication, speech and debate on a broad range of social and even political matters."[83]

— Bret Taylor, Facebook's chief technology officer.

Because no clear consensus exists, many call for broad, general legislation that would protect privacy. As Clippinger sums it up: "Now is the time to get the rules of the road right so that it is possible to both protect and share valuable and sensitive information. This does not require government micro-regulation, but it does require some thoughtful regulation, principles and architectures that create the right checks and balances."[82]

A Forum for Public Communication

Many believe that Congress should be cautious in crafting laws to govern social media as regulation could impede the open exchange of information. As Facebook's chief technology officer, Bret Taylor testified before Congress in 2010: "Facebook and other social technologies are increasingly important forums for public communication, speech and debate on a broad range of social and even political matters. Our country's traditions appropriately include a great hesitancy to regulate communication and the sharing of information in such areas."[83]

The global nature of the Internet fosters additional—and unique—considerations. For instance, laws in the United States would still allow people in other countries to disclose and disseminate potentially sensitive data about a person regardless of the person's country of origin. For all of these reasons, many feel that the creation of additional laws would do little to tackle all of the challenges related to privacy. Rather, users whose data has been compromised should tap into existing legislation that already protects privacy directly and that would allow users to file suit if necessary.

How society should respond to the current trend toward online sharing and openness—and the diminished privacy that results—remains unclear. As users learn to navigate a digital world that "puts you in a public square with a surveillance camera turned on,"[84] as Sherry Turkle puts it, the debate is certain to intensify.

Facts

- Facial recognition technology can link a photo of a Facebook user to a different photo of the same person on an unrelated site, where the individual may have wanted their identity secret.

- In 2007 Facebook debuted a feature called Beacon that disclosed what users bought on the web. It was pulled after users deemed it a privacy violation.

- Many social network sites have been sued in Europe, which has stronger privacy laws than the United States.

- In 2010 users worried about privacy organized a Quit Facebook Day. The event attracted 37,000 of Facebook's then 500 million members.

- A British study revealed that 92 percent of Twitter users were willing to accept friend requests from complete strangers, giving them access to their personal information.

Related Organizations and Websites

American Library Association (ALA)
50 E. Huron St.
Chicago, IL 60611
phone: (800) 545-2433
fax: (312) 440-9374
e-mail: ala@ala.org
website: www.ala.org

The ALA was founded in 1876 to provide leadership for the development, promotion, and improvement of library and information services and ensure access to information for all. It is opposed to censorship in all forms. The association's website provides information about legislation that affects Internet access at public libraries.

Berkman Center for Internet & Society
Harvard University
23 Everett St., 2nd Floor
Cambridge, MA 02138
phone: (617) 495-7547
fax: (617) 495-7641
e-mail: cyber@law.harvard.edu
website: http://cyber.law.harvard.edu

The Berkman Center for Internet & Society was founded in 1997 to explore and understand cyberspace and help pioneer its development. To this end, the Berkman Center conducts research on a wide variety of issues related to the Internet, including privacy, politics, law, and culture. Many publications are available on the center's website, including the 2010 report *Youth, Privacy, and Reputation.*

Center for Democracy and Technology (CDT)

1631 I St. NW, Suite 1100
Washington, DC 20006
phone: (202) 637-9800
fax: (202) 637-0968
e-mail: info@cdt.org
website: www.cdt.org

The CDT is a nonprofit civil liberties organization dedicated to keeping the Internet and all new communications media open, innovative, and free. The CDT works to promote its goals through research and education. Publications available on the website include press releases, position statements, and numerous reports related to free expression.

Center for Safe and Responsible Internet Use

474 W. 29th Ave.
Eugene, OR 97405
phone: (541) 556-1145
e-mail: contact@csriu.org
website: www.cyberbully.org

The Center for Safe and Responsible Internet Use was founded by Nancy Willard, an expert on student use of the Internet. The center offers numerous reports and guides designed to address the challenges related to managing web technologies in the schools. Its new program, Embracing Digital Youth, seeks to ensure that all young people become "cyber savvy" as they learn to navigate the digital world.

Electronic Frontier Foundation (EFF)

454 Shotwell St.
San Francisco, CA 94110-1914
phone: (415) 436-9333
e-mail: information@eff.org
website: www.eff.org

The EFF is an organization of students, lawyers, policy analysts, and others who seek to foster awareness of telecommunications issues as they relate to civil liberties, including the right to free speech and privacy in the digital world. The group brings and defends lawsuits to preserve First Amendment rights in all telecommunications technologies.

Electronic Privacy Information Center (EPIC)

1718 Connecticut Ave. NW, Suite 200
Washington, DC 20009
phone: (202) 483-1140
fax: (202) 483-1248
website: http://epic.org

EPIC is a research center founded in 1994 to focus public attention on civil liberty issues involving the Internet and emerging digital technologies. The website offers news and information on a variety of topics, including children's online privacy, social networking, and Facebook.

Federal Trade Commission (FTC)

600 Pennsylvania Ave. NW
Washington, DC 20580
phone: (202) 326-2222
website: www.ftc.gov

The FTC is the consumer protection agency of the federal government. It deals with many issues that pertain to economics, including unfair and illegal business practices and identity theft on the Internet. Its website includes numerous publications about how to safely use the Internet and digital technologies.

Focus on the Family

Colorado Springs, CO 80995
phone: (800) 232-6459
website: www.family.org

Focus on the Family is a global Christian ministry dedicated to helping families thrive while preserving biblical beliefs. To this end, the organization provides numerous guidelines on topics such as parenting, relationships, marriage, and social issues. The project Focus on Your Child provides instructive materials to help parents address issues associated with social networking and Internet safety.

GetNetWise

e-mail: cmatsuda@neted.org
website: www.getnetwise.org

GetNetWise is a public service coalition provided by Internet industry corporations and public interest organizations to help ensure that Internet users have safe online experiences. The website offers articles on many topics, including online child safety, privacy, and social networking.

Internet Education Foundation (IEF)

Center for Democracy and Technology
1634 I St. NW, Suite 1100
Washington, DC 20006
phone: (202) 638-4370
fax: (202) 637-0968
e-mail: tim@neted.org
website: www.neted.org

The IEF is a nonprofit organization founded in 1996 that supports privacy, free expression, and other civil liberties as they relate to the Internet. To this end, the foundation works to inform policy making on Internet-related issues both in government and the private sector. It also seeks to educate the public about the challenges presented by the Internet and to offer solutions.

Internet Society (ISOC)

1775 Wiehle Ave., Suite 201
Reston, VA 20190-5108
phone: (703) 439-2120
fax: (703) 326-9881
e-mail: isoc@isoc.org
website: www.isoc.org

The ISOC is an international nonprofit group founded in 1992 to provide leadership in the formation of Internet-related standards, education, and public policy. Its goal is to ensure the open development of the Internet for the benefit of people throughout the world. The ISOC acts as a global clearinghouse for Internet information and educational materials.

Wired Safety

e-mail: webmaster@wiredsafety.org
website: www.wiredsafety.org

Wired Safety is a nonprofit group founded in 1995 to promote online safety and education. The group has more than 9,000 volunteers who operate online to provide help and resources to victims of cybercrime and harassment. Wired Safety provides extensive information on all aspects of cyberspace safety, privacy, and security issues.

Additional Reading

Books

Mark Bauerlein, *The Digital Divide: Arguments For and Against Facebook, Google, Texting, and the Age of Social Networking.* New York: Tarcher, 2011.

Nicholas Carr, *The Shallows: What the Internet Is Doing to Our Brains.* New York: W.W. Norton, 2011.

Robert Fine, ed., *The Big Book of Social Media: Case Studies, Stories, Perspectives.* Tulsa, OK: Yorkshire, 2010.

Todd Kelsey, *Social Networking Spaces: From Facebook to Twitter and Everything in Between.* New York: Apress, 2010.

David Kirkpatrick, *The Facebook Effect: The Inside Story of the Company That Is Connecting the World.* New York: Simon and Schuster, 2010.

Evgeny Morozov, *The Net Delusion: The Dark Side of Internet Freedom.* New York: PublicAffairs, 2011.

John Palfrey, *Born Digital: Understanding the First Generation of Digital Natives.* New York: Basic Books, 2010.

Don Tapscott, *Wikinomics: How Mass Collaboration Changes Everything.* New York: Portfolio Trade, 2010.

Sherry Turkle, *Alone Together: Why We Expect More from Technology and Less from Each Other.* New York: Basic Books, 2011.

D.E. Wittkower, *Facebook and Philosophy: What's on Your Mind?* Chicago: Open Court, 2010.

Deanna Zandt, *Share This! How You Will Change the World with Social Networking*. San Francisco: Berrett-Koehler, 2010.

Periodicals

Chris Anderson and Michael Wolff, "The Web Is Dead," *Wired*, September 2010.

Larry Carlat, "Confessions of a Tweeter," *New York Times Magazine*, November 11, 2011.

Dalton Conley, "Wired for Distraction: Kids and Social Media," *Time*, February 21, 2011.

Greg Ferenstein, "Three Ways Educators Are Embracing Social Technology," Mashable, January 10, 2010. www.mashable .com.

Dan Fletcher, "How Facebook Is Redefining Privacy," *Time*, May 20, 2010.

Guilbert Gates, "Facebook Privacy: A Bewildering Tangle of Options," *New York Times*, May 12, 2010.

Malcolm Gladwell, "Small Change: Why the Revolution Will Not Be Tweeted," *New Yorker*, October 4, 2010.

Megan Harris, "Social Networking Sites Dominate Users' Social Lives," *Lancaster (PA) Intelligencer Journal*, April 3, 2010.

Sarah Kessler, "The Case for Social Media in Schools," Mashable, September 29, 2010. www.mashable.com.

Harry McCracken, "Did Facebook Just Change Social Networking Forever?," *Time*, September 29, 2011.

Tom Meltzer, "Social Networking: Failure to Connect: How Can You Be Lonely When You Have So Many Friends?," *Guardian*, August 7, 2010. www.guardian.co.uk.

Lisa Pevtzow, "How Common Is Web Addiction?," *Chicago Tribune*, August 13, 2010.

Carol Polsky, "Social Sites a Big Teen Temptation," *Newsday*, March 28, 2010.

Jennifer Preston, "Protestors Look for Ways to Feed the Web," *New York Times*, November 24, 2011.

Matt Richtel, "Hooked on Gadgets, and Paying a Mental Price," *New York Times*, June 6, 2010.

Michael Robertson, "Is Privacy History?," *San Diego Union-Tribune*, November 13, 2011.

Zachary Romano, "Why We Love Social Networking," *Syracuse (NY) Post Standard*, March 1, 2010.

Jeffrey Rosen, "The Web Means the End of Forgetting," *New York Times Magazine*, July 19, 2010.

John Timpane, "Tweeting, Blogging, and E-Mailing Our Way to More Fulfilling Personal Lives," *Newark (NJ) Star-Ledger*, January 10, 2010.

Source Notes

Introduction: A Communication Revolution

1. Clay Shirky, "How Social Media Can Make History," TED Talks, June 2009. www.ted.com.

2. Shirky, "How Social Media Can Make History."

Chapter One: What Are the Origins of the Social Networking Debate?

3. Quoted in Michael Simon, "The Complete History of Social Networking—CBBS to Twitter,"MacLife.com, December 14, 2009. www.maclife.com.

4. Dan Conger, interview by author, November 30, 2011.

5. Quoted in David Kirkpatrick, *The Facebook Effect: The Inside Story of the Company That Is Connecting the World.* New York: Simon & Schuster, 2011, p. 107.

6. Quoted in Christopher Maag, "Internet Hoax That Turned Fatal Draws Anger but No Charges," *New York Times*, November 28, 2007. www.nytimes.com.

7. Kimling Lam, "Occupy Wall Street: Social and Mainstream Media," *Meltwater* (blog). http://blog.meltwater.com.

Chapter Two: Is Social Networking Changing the Nature of Relationships?

8. John Cacioppo, *Loneliness: Human Nature and the Need for Social Connection.* New York: W.W. Norton, 2008, p. 5.

9. Quoted in Cacioppo, *Loneliness*, p. 7.

10. June Cohen, "The Rise of Social Media Is Really a Reprise," in *Is the Internet Changing the Way You Think?* John Brockman, ed. New York: HarperCollins, 2011, p. 39.

11. Bill Keller, "Bill Keller Responds to My Objections to His Comments About Social Media," *Technosociology: Our Tools, Ourselves* (blog), June 23, 2011. technosociology.org.

12. Quoted in Socialmediatoday, "Why Dunbar's Number Is Irrelevant," January 25, 2010. www.socialmediatoday.com.

13. Quoted in Ebony Wheeldon, "A Social Society: The Positive Effects of Communicating Through Social Networking Sites," Online Conference on Networks and Communities, April 25, 2010. http://networkconference.netstudies.org.

14. Quoted in Webtribes, "Can Social Networking Benefit Your Mental Health?," April 2008. www.webtribes.com.

15. Quoted in Pew Internet and American Life Project, "The Future of Social Relations," July 2010. www.pewinternet.org.

16. Quoted in Wheeldon, "A Social Society."

17. Quoted in Caroline Lyders, "Social Networking and Loneliness: Research Finds Link Between Online Life and Depression," TBD, February 3, 2011. www.tbd.com.

18. Quoted in Sharon Jayson, "'Flocking' Behavior Lands on Social Networking Sites," *USA Today*, September 28, 2009. www.usatoday.com.

19. Quoted in Jayson, "'Flocking' Behavior Lands on Social Networking Sites."

20. Quoted in Sherry Turkle, *Alone Together: Why We Expect More from Technology and Less from Each Other.* New York: Basic Books, 2011, p. 164.

21. Turkle, *Alone Together*, p. 172.

22. Danah Boyd, "Social Media Is Here to Stay, Now What?," speech at Microsoft Research Tech Fest, February 26, 2009. www.danah.org.

23. Turkle, *Alone Together*, p. 153.

24. Quoted in Turkle, *Alone Together*, p. 184.

25. Quoted in Turkle, *Alone Together,* p. 181.

26. Cohen, "The Rise of Social Media Is Really a Reprise."

Chapter Three: How Has Social Networking Impacted Political and International Events?

27. Shirky, "How Social Media Can Make History."

28. Sascha Segan, "Learning from Iran's Twitter Revolution," *PC Magazine*, August 2009. www.pcmag.com.

29. José Antonio Vargas, "Egypt, the Age of Disruption and the 'Me' in Media," *Huffington Post*, February 7, 2011. www.huff ingtonpost.com.

30. Quoted in Kirkpatrick, *The Facebook Effect*, p. 288.

31. Quoted in Joel Schectman, "Iran's Twitter Revolution? Maybe Not Yet*,*" *Business Week*, June 18, 2009. www.businessweek .com.

32. Quoted in Schectman, "Iran's Twitter Revolution? Maybe Not Yet."

33. Quoted in Schectman, "Iran's Twitter Revolution? Maybe Not Yet."

34. Quoted in Catharine Smith, "Egypt's Facebook Revolution: Wael Ghonim Thanks the Social Network," *Huffington Post*, November 30, 2011. www.huffingtonpost.com.

35. Malcolm Gladwell, "Does Egypt Need Twitter?," *New Yorker*, February 2, 2011. www.newyorker.com.

36. Evgeny Morozov, *The Net Delusion: The Dark Side of Internet Freedom*. New York: PublicAffairs, 2011, p. 261.

37. Morozov, *The Net Delusion*, p. 264.

38. Morozov, *The Net Delusion*, p. 264.

39. Don Tapscott, *Grown Up Digital: How the Net Generation Is Changing Your World*. New York: McGraw-Hill, 2009, p. 247.

40. Quoted in Justin Mullins, "How Crowd-Sourcing Has Helped in Haiti," *New Scientist*, January 30, 2010. www.newscientist .com.

41. ScicnceDaily, "Social Media Poised to Drive Disaster Preparedness and Response," July 28, 2011. www.sciencedaily.com.

42. Charlotte Tucker, "Social Media, Texting Play New Role in Response to Disasters," *Nation's Health*, May/June 2011. www.thenationshealth.org.

43. Quoted in Tomoko A. Hosaka, "Japan Disaster Sparks Social Media Innovation," *Huffington Post*, March 31, 2011. www.huffingtonpost.com.

Chapter Four: How Does Social Networking Affect Education and the Workplace?

44. Nicholas Carr, "Is Google Making Us Stupid?," *Atlantic*, July/August 2008. www.theatlantic.com.

45. Nicholas Carr, "The Bookless Library," in *Is the Internet Changing the Way You Think?* John Brockman, ed. New York: HarperCollins, 2011, p. 2.

46. Turkle, *Alone Together*, p. 169.

47. Quoted in Elias Aboujaoude, *Virtually You: The Dangerous Powers of the E-Personality*. New York: W.W. Norton, 2011, p. 192.

48. Quoted in Richard Watson, *Future Minds: How the Digital Age Is Changing Our Minds, Why This Matters and What We Can Do About It*. London: Nicholas Brealey, 2010, p. 20.

49. Tapscott, *Grown Up Digital*, p.117.

50. Quoted in *UM News*, "Educational Benefits of Social Networking Sites," July 10, 2008. www.1umn.edu.

51. Tapscott, *Grown Up Digital*, p. 127.

52. Quoted in Michelle R. Davis, "Social Networking Goes to School," *Digital Directions*, June 14, 2010. www.edweek.org.

53. Quoted in Meris Stansbury, "Ten Ways Schools Are Using Social Media Effectively," *eSchool News*, October 21, 2011. www.eschoolnews.com.

54. Turkle, *Alone Together*, p. 227.

55. Martin Lindstrom, "You Love Your iPhone. Literally," *New York Times*, September 30, 2011. www.nytimes.com.

56. Quoted in Sarah Schweizer, "No Easy Fix Found for Bullying," *Boston Globe*, December 30, 2010. www.bostonglobe.com.

57. Jeanne C. Meister and Karie Willyerd, "The Uber-Connected Organization: A Mandate for 2010," *Harvard Business Review* (blog), November 11, 2009. blogs.hbr.org.

58. David DiSalvo, "Are Social Networks Messing with Your Head?," *Scientific American Mind*, December 29, 2009.

59. Quoted in Turkle, *Alone Together*, p. 227.

60. *ComputerWorld UK*, "Four Ways Social Networking Can Boost Your Employees' Productivity," July 25, 2011. www.computerworlduk.com.

61. Quoted in Peter Dockrill, "Why Social Media in the Workplace Is Not the Enemy: Business Benefits of Staff Usage," *APC*, December 1, 2011. apcmag.com.

62. Quoted in Turkle, *Alone Together*, p.165.

63. Quoted in Turkle, *Alone Together*, p.166.

64. Quoted in Kirkpatrick, *The Facebook Effect*, p. 199.

Chapter Five: Does Social Networking Pose a Threat to Privacy?

65. Clive Thompson, "Brave New World of Digital Intimacy," *New York Times*, September 7, 2008. www.nytimes.com.

66. Seirian Sumner, "By Changing My Behavior," in *Is the Internet Changing the Way You Think?* John Brockman, ed. p. 198.

67. Quoted in Thompson, "Brave New World of Digital Intimacy."

68. Quoted in Pew Internet & American Life Project, "Millenials Will Make Online Sharing in Networks a Lifelong Habit," July 2010. www.pewinternet.org.

69. Quoted in Morozov, *The Net Delusion*, p. 223.

70. Thompson, "Brave New World of Digital Intimacy."

71. Djana, "'A Race of Peeping Toms': Facebook Stalking and Geo-Location," August 15, 2010, djanak.wordpress.com.

72. Ben Parr, "In Defense of Facebook," *Mashable*, May 16, 2010. www.mashable.com.

73. Kirkpatrick, *The Facebook Effect*, p. 204.

74. Quoted in Aboujaoude, *Virtually You: The Dangerous Powers of the E-Personality*, p. 248.

75. Quoted in Kirkpatrick, *The Facebook Effect*, p. 205.

76. Parr, "In Defense of Facebook."

77. Quoted in Tapscott, *Grown Up Digital*, p. 65.

78. Joel Stein, "Your Data, Yourself," *Time*, March 21, 2011. www.time.com.

79. Quoted in Tapscott, *Grown Up Digital*, p. 65.

80. John Clippinger, "Facebook Is Betting Against Its Users," *Harvard Law School* (blog), June 4, 2010. blogs.law.harvard.edu.

81. Quoted in Marcia Clemmitt, "Social Networking," *CQ Researcher*, September 17, 2010. www.cqpress.com.

82. Clippinger, "Facebook Is Betting Against Its Users."

83. Bret Taylor, testimony before Senate Committee on Commerce, Science, and Transportation, July 27, 2010. www.gpo.gov.

84. Turkle, *Alone Together*, p. 243.

Index

About the Authors

Bonnie Szumski has been an editor and author of nonfiction books for 25 years. Jill Karson has been an editor and author of nonfiction books for young adults for 15 years.